my Name was MUSHROOM

My Life as a Teenage Runaway in The Source Family Commune

WENDY BAKER
and BRIAN SOLON

Think It Publishing

My Name Was Mushroom:
My Life as a Teenage Runaway in The Source Family Commune

Wendy Baker and Brian Solon

Published by Think It Publishing

Think It Publishing
Email: MushroomAquarian@gmail.com

Limit of Liability/Disclaimer of Warranty:

Publishing team: Author Bridge Media, www.AuthorBridgeMedia.com
Publishing Manager: Laurie Aranda
Cover Designer: Peri Gabriel

Library of Congress Control Number: 2022908909
ISBN: 978-0-9960552-6-0—softcover
ISBN: 978-0-9960552-7-7—hardcover
ISBN: 978-0-9960552-8-4—ebook
ISBN: 978-0-9960552-9-1—audio

Ordering Information:

Quantity sales. Special discounts are available on quantity purchases by corporations, associations, and others. For details, contact the publisher at MushroomAquarian@gmail.com.

Printed in the United States of America.

DEDICATION

To the love of my life and soul mate, Bart Baker, who has given me the ultimate support for over 44 years. I couldn't have written this book without you.

A special dedication to my mother, Norma, who has passed away. And to my father-in-law, Jim Baker, and mother-in-law, Elaine Baker: my love for you is unmeasurable.

CONTENTS

ACKNOWLEDGMENTS

I am eternally grateful for my Source Family experience. It has made a positive difference in my life. I love my Source Family brothers and sisters who made this journey with me. Thank you to Jim Baker, also known as Yahowah, my spiritual father, father-in-law, and teacher: you taught me how to live my life in a positive and loving way. I will never forget you.

Thank you to my three children: my daughter Jaime, a.k.a. Stardust, and son-in-law Jason Black; my daughter Amber Baker and daughter-in-law Patti Palafox; and my son Brian Baker and daughter-in-law Sarah. And to my four grandsons: Julian and Luca Calvo; Jonah and Jacob Black.

Thank you to my friends in Malibu who encouraged me to write this story about my life as a youth: Robin and Greg Windham; Gail and Sam Seelig; Patty and Jerry Seymour; Linda Fleidermen; Betty and Bill Cacciatore; Rosalie Shore; Howard Rosenberg; Doug Olen, my tennis coach; and all my tennis friends at Malibu Racquet Club.

Thank you to my brother- and sister-in-law Ben and Carla Baker for giving me their blessings. And to my sister-in-law Celeste, a.k.a. Tau, Baker, and my nieces: Tia Lutz, Onka, a.k.a. Amanda Scott, and her husband, John Scott, June Scott and Amanda Baker.

Thank you to my Aquarian Family who supported me: Damian, a.k.a. Bob Paul; Sunflower, a.k.a. Patrick Burke; Heaven, a.k.a. Nancy Hirsch; Sir Knight, a.k.a. Peter Tobin; Paralda, a.k.a. Elizabeth Keller; Blessing, a.k.a. Marci Gossard; Goddess, a.k.a. Mary Blyth; Waterfall, a.k.a. Ian Blyth; Dawn, a.k.a. Hurwitz; Anastasia, a.k.a. Ellie Zacks; Joshua Kemp, Katina; and all my brothers and sisters in the Source Family.

A special thank you to Scott Schwimer, my attorney, for adding fun and flare to this book and for believing in me and my story.

A huge thank you to Helen Chang at Author Bridge Media for putting on the finishing touches. And to Laurie Aranda for helping me publish the book.

Thank you to Alex Koch, audio engineer.

I owe gratitude to Brian Solon, my co-writer and inspiration in writing my story; for taking this journey with me and sharing all of his wisdom.

I am beyond grateful to my love and husband of 44 years. Bart has motivated me and inspired me to write this story. I could not have written these words without his support and blessings.

Chapter 1

RUNAWAY

The Force Within

Spring 1972

My moment of truth happened one night at the age of 14 as I sat on the edge of my bed in the dark with my sister sleeping next to me. I was trembling with fear and bursting with excitement, trying to figure out which one was going to win. Should I go to morning meditation?

I was supposed to go to school and had a big test that I'd been studying for all week. I was always a good student. I started losing interest in school by the seventh grade and never gained back my enthusiasm that I once had. I was bored. I wasn't being stimulated. The education wasn't exciting for me anymore. I didn't want to memorize dates of wars and presidents. It no longer made sense to me.

I gravitated towards spirituality. Who am I and where am I going? I wanted to learn—who is Buddha? Who are the Yogi masters of the world? How could nutrition affect my health and my body? I was always active and saw exercise as an ingredient

1

of a balanced life. I didn't know enough about it and I craved learning how the body works.

These topics were never discussed in my family. No one in my family went to college, so I thought that was not an option. I was told early on that I was to get a job as a secretary.

My thoughts changed suddenly. I had gone from being a good student to socializing with the hippies in school. Many of my peers did drugs, but I wasn't one of them. I didn't do drugs or alcohol, and never touched a cigarette. Deep down inside I was a good girl. I always craved knowledge of life.

As school became boring I got involved with ditching and hanging out with the Laurel Canyon gang. The Laurel Canyon group ditched a lot and would get together at different houses smoking pot and having sex. I didn't fit this category but I was intrigued by all of this. It was fun to go against the rules and do something that was not so perfect, because I was always expected to be the 'brain' in the family. I observed their behavior and participated in a mild way.

I hated being out of control. Typically I had one boyfriend and could stay away from most of the trouble. It was like I had angels guiding me and keeping me sane. I do believe we are destined to travel on the path chosen for us.

What would my sisters do when they woke up and noticed that I was gone? It was a scary thought and concerned me. How would my Mom react? Would they even care?

I was the third of four sisters all born a year apart—while we were close in age, we otherwise weren't exactly close with one another. Our Dad wasn't in the picture (I had never even met him—and mom never talked about him) and our single mom was not the greatest mother—there were no hugs, kisses, or even simple recognition. Zilch.

High school was becoming a nightmare and in many ways the wider world seemed to be falling apart. It was 1972 and many people in my generation were strung out on drugs, or on the verge of being drafted to fight in the Vietnam War, or feeling totally directionless. I knew I didn't belong there and was seeking a new path. The thought of that change was terrifying.

Everyone in my life—my mom, my sisters, and all my friends—had begged me to not join "the cult." But there was no stopping me. I made the decision to take a leap of faith and join the Source Family. There was a strong force within me to take this path. As the clock approached 3:30 a.m., I snuck out my second-story bedroom window, slid down a vine, and jumped into a blue and white VW van. I was wearing a white dress and had left all my other clothes and possessions behind—no makeup, no purse, no ID. I had no idea that I was never going back home again.

Ramacharaka drove us to the Temple on Sunset Boulevard to rendezvous with Jim and Robin, then we all caravanned to The Mother House in Los Feliz Estates where morning meditation began at 4 a.m.

On the way there, Robin was driving the van as Jim sat in front. I sat behind Robin, feeling euphoric and special that I got to have that precious time with them on the 20-minute drive from Sweetzer and Sunset to the Hollywood Hills. Jim was wearing white pants, a white shirt, a shawl, and sandals. Robin wore a beautiful white dress with a beaded sash belt and birkenstocks. I was in awe of her beauty—beautiful brown hair and big brown eyes. She was singing all the way there. I felt so special being in that car with them. Outside it was chilly and dark and there were a zillion stars. I was only 14 and yet I felt like a free spirit on a path that I believed in for the first time in my life.

Pond Raiders

Three Years Earlier

A few years earlier I was introduced to The Source Family, founded by Jim Baker at The Source Restaurant in the heart of LA's Sunset Strip in 1969. I originally met Jim Baker through his son Bart Baker, who I met purely by chance.

Early one Saturday morning my younger sister and I were roller-skating down La Cienega Boulevard to The Islander restaurant. Outside of The Islander was a small pond beneath an arch bridge where people threw in coins and made a wish.

Our plan that day, as every Saturday, was to retrieve coins from the pond and use them to buy candy at Rexall Drug Store. Should we secure a sufficient amount of sunken treasure, we might also hang out for a while at Kiddieland Amusement Park before returning home. It was a magical place, with a Ferris Wheel, racecars, a roller coaster, and more. Lots of celebrities brought their children there. Right next door was Pony Land where kids could saddle up and ride little ponies.

However it was not to pass. As we approached the pond, we noticed two boys already on the scene, fishing out coins for themselves. My sister Janice assertively announced our arrival.

"Hey, this is *our* pond. What are you doing here?"

We all stopped and stared at each other. The boys were unfazed and held their ground.

"Nope, this is actually OUR pond."

Then I noticed the cute boy with blonde hair and the biggest blue eyes. I was immediately taken with him. He seemed so grown up and confident. Was it love (like I even knew what that meant)? It kind of scared me. My heart was beating fast and I didn't know why.

The next thing I knew, the blonde haired boy and his friend gave chase, but thanks to our roller skates, we gained a slight speed advantage rolling up La Cienega back towards our apartment building on 505 North Alfred Street. The boys pursued and playfully taunted us as we skated for our lives. At last we reached our apartment building, where we ditched our roller skates outside and ran upstairs to our third-floor balcony, overlooking an alley across from Norm's restaurant. The boys soon arrived and called at us on the balcony from the alley below.

"Hey, come down, we just want to talk to you!"

They were kind of cute, especially the one with long blonde hair, but they were complete strangers. We stayed safely upstairs and after a while they eventually disappeared. The next morning, we realized that our roller skates had also mysteriously disappeared.

In Trouble With Tiki

Spring 1969

Fast-forward to a few months later, my best friend Tiki (age 14) and I (age 12) were out on one of our many hitchhiking adventures. Tiki was exotic-looking with long black hair, pale skin, and piercing blue eyes. Standing out by the road with a thumb up, wearing hip-hugger jeans with a big belt, bell bottoms, and a tight shirt, it seldom took long for us to get noticed and picked up by passersby and driven most of the way towards our intended destination.

That day Tiki and I hitchhiked to Lookout Mountain in Laurel Canyon, where we made our way up a long unmarked dirt driveway and found ourselves at Parker's House—a slightly run-down hippie haven populated by about a half-dozen teenagers smoking pot and listening to music, presided over by Parker, who was easily twice or three-times our age, and the lurking presence of his creepy, somewhat nasty mother (aka Grandma).

Tiki's boyfriend Tommy had invited us to meet the Laurel Canyon gang and said that he would be there. Shortly after arriving on the scene, I was hanging out in the guest house area clad in tight bell-bottom jeans and a crepe shirt with long sleeves and buttons down the front when a boy wearing a fringe leather jacket and cowboy boots approached me.

"Have we met somewhere before?" he asked.

He looked familiar and I tried to place him.

"Are you that girl from the pond at The Islander, with your sister?"

I couldn't believe it. "Wait, that was you?" My heart started beating faster.

His hair was now longer and straighter, and he was dressed differently, but it was definitely him, the cute blonde guy, one of the daring duo who had chased me and my sister and ruined our plans to buy candy and hit Kiddieland. It was love at second sight. Within minutes of recollecting our prior episode the romance began.

We talked like we'd known each other a long time. I felt so strange in his presence. I'd never met anyone like him before. He talked with so much confidence. This physical attraction was immediate and some making out might have happened. I'm not sure if I had ever kissed a boy before. He definitely seemed knowledgeable in the kissing department, and then some. I felt a little scared and wasn't sure how to handle him. I quickly set boundaries and slowed him down. I thought this would either end our budding relationship, or he would honor my prudeness.

After spending the day there with Tiki and the blonde boy—Bart Baker—I was smitten. If there's such a thing as love at age 12, this could be it. Later that afternoon Parker drove us back down the hill in his funky van and brought me home. I had given Bart my phone number and he started calling me—a lot. We soon became increasingly inseparable, and he was constantly coming over to my house and I was going over to his—taking lots of taxis rides back and forth, or having my mom take me up to his house and later pick me up.

Bart lived in a Spanish-style house at 8145 Mulholland Drive in Laurel Canyon with his mother Elaine (who was married to Bart's dad Jim Baker for 15 years) and two brothers—Beau, who was around 17, and Ben, who was about 6 1/2. Ben always hung out with us and was absolutely adorable. We all called him Benny. Beau was like a rebel—in a motorcycle gang, always getting into trouble. He was emotionally handicapped and hearing impaired. He was difficult for Bart to live with, often violent and angry.

Bart's mom Elaine was a beautiful woman, always dressed to the nines. She was a graduate of the Pasadena Art Center and University of Washington, Seattle. Reminiscent of Doris Day and Debbie Reynolds. Other occupants of the house included full-time housekeeper, Maria, and Jean & Jerome—a couple of hippies who worked on special projects in the house, often getting high and sometimes watching the kids—and two German shepherds, Blackie and Pandie.

Many of our dates were Bart taking me out to dinner at The Aware Inn—the gourmet organic restaurant at 8828 Sunset Boulevard owned and run by Bart's mom Elaine Baker in West Hollywood on the Sunset Strip between Larrabee and Holloway, across from Tower Records—an elegantly designed upscale dinner house.

It was like a hideaway for celebrities. The Aware Inn's very first guest was Greta Garbo. Everybody went there—JFK, Warren Beatty, Anthony Perkins, Steve McQueen, Tuesday Weld, Paul Newman, Joanne Woodward, Marlon Brando, Shirley McLaine, Carol Burnett, Debbie Reynolds. And the list goes on. The upstairs private dining room had a majestic view of Sunset Blvd.

Bart (age 12) would be ordering the most exquisite dishes on the menu like escargot or filet mignon. I was far less adventurous, ordering an Aware Salad or a plain baked potato with butter. I didn't know what I was missing. But Bart knew, and he made it his mission to educate me about the many wonders of the culinary sphere. Over time, I would learn the delights of stuffed mushrooms, scampi, and chocolate cheesecake.

Going out to eat with Bart was an introduction to a whole new world. Back at my house, my sisters and I barely subsisted on a totally uninspirational diet. Every Sunday afternoon my Mom would pile us into the station wagon and drive us (while chain-smoking) to the grocery store, where she would have each of us pick out seven frozen TV dinners for our upcoming week's selections. 28 frozen TV dinners in the grocery cart.

After the grocery store, sometimes we'd 'splurge' and go to McDonald's for a hamburger, fries, and a shake, or Thrifty's for a 5-cent ice cream scoop. In our household, food was more a means of survival versus something to be actually enjoyed. Or cooked. Much less nutritious.

When Bart visited my house, he looked in our freezer and was astounded by what he saw—stacks and stacks of TV dinners. Peering into our pantry, he saw little more than canned foods, prompting him to ask me, "What's going on here?" I thought everyone ate like this. I had never heard of fresh organic foods.

Bart decided he had to show my family another way of eating. When he came over to our house and cooked a meal for my entire family, sisters, Mom and all—everyone quickly warmed up to Bart. Maybe that's why my Mom pretended not to notice when Bart would come over to my house at night and sneak into my second story bedroom window. Bart would be hiding under the covers when my Mom came to the door, saying: "Turn off the lights, go to bed."

Bart would work on the weekends at The Aware Inn, starting at 10pm making their celebrated all-organic ice cream. This was something I had to see. We would go on dates making ice cream together, often consuming quite a lot in the process. Sometimes other friends would come over and join us, a few beers might appear, bowls were passed around, and good times were had.

Meeting Jim Baker

Summer 1969

After we'd been dating for about a month, Bart brought me to The Source Restaurant for lunch on a Saturday to meet his Dad, Jim Baker, for the first time. Jim had opened The Source Restaurant at 8301 Sunset Boulevard on April 1, 1969. The building was made of brick, which Bart proudly told me he had helped his Dad build, brick by brick. Patrons dined both indoors and on an outside patio, enjoying vegetarian health foods, fresh squeezed juices, and desserts made with honey.

Bart prepared me for the meeting, saying, "Don't be threatened. He's not the average father." Bart was very sweet, holding my hand as we walked inside. The first time I saw Jim Baker, I could barely talk. Standing 6-foot-5, he was tall and handsome—a huge presence, built of solid muscle—intimidating and mesmerizing at the same time. I remember his gorgeous sea blue eyes and being stunned by his magnetism. I had never met anyone close to looking like him. His hair was a mixture of brown and blonde, with a touch of gray—long and curly. He was a gentle, loving giant. If he resembled anyone, he looked like Jesus Christ.

"Dad, I want to introduce you to my girlfriend Wendy," Bart said.

Jim warmly took my hand between his two hands, so loving with a huge smile. I had never felt such loving hands before. It was life-changing to experience any kind of love from a stranger. It made my heart warm and sent a sensation far beyond anything I'd ever known. I wondered if this was normal or was I imagining this feeling. Needless to say I couldn't stop thinking about my sensational encounter.

"You have good taste, son. Wendy, it is very nice to meet you. I have good taste too. This is Robin. Please, sit down." What softened the whole experience was his girlfriend Robin, sitting beside him. I quickly started to relax and enjoy the conversation.

Our Saturday lunch must have gone well, because a few days later Bart suggested, "Let's go to my Dad's place for dinner." I couldn't wait to see Jim Baker again to see if I was still feeling this sensation. For our dinner date at The Source we would dine with Jim and his girlfriend Robin. Bart and I ordered the Source Special, an open face sandwich with avocado, alfalfa sprouts, mushrooms, melted cheddar cheese with sprinkles of sesame seeds on top and garnished with grated beets and carrots with the Source dressing. This would soon become one of my favorite dishes of all time—mouth-watering deliciousness.

At that time, Jim and Robin were temporarily living in a van in the parking lot behind The Source Restaurant while Jim built a new room above the restaurant which would become their bedroom and home. I thought it was so cool that they lived in a van.

That evening as Bart and I walked into The Source Restaurant, we saw Jim and Robin, both wearing all white clothes and leather sandals (which he made by hand), seated in the corner table beside a fireplace with multicolored candle wax dripping and flowing down the sides. Bart approached his father and embraced him with a hug. At first I was kind of taken aback—this kind of affectionate display was so foreign to me, coming from my upbringing where Dad wasn't around and Mom never expressed any kind of love to us.

Jim and Robin had the cutest relationship. Jim was much older than Robin (he was approaching 50), but it worked. Robin, in her early 20s, was beautiful, with curly flowing brown hair, gorgeous big brown eyes, and a perfect body. She was full of love. Robin was very playful with Jim and he seemed to love the attention. They looked like soul mates to me. Deeply in love in perfect peace and harmony. I enjoyed being around their energy. At dinner together we were discussing life, food, spirituality. It was the first time in my life I felt love and peacefulness.

We all hit it off, and afterwards we started to all go out together as a group—me, Bart, Jim, and Robin, joined frequently by Bart's little brother Ben—and go on adventures, often to the movies. Sometimes we traveled together in Jim's van, sometimes we took a taxi, and sometimes we would walk, no matter if the theater was 15 minutes or two hours away. Walking with Jim Baker was a workout. He was so tall and we were all a full foot shorter. I practically had to jog to keep up with him, as we all did. This was a happy time for me.

When Jim and Robin got married in May 1970, Bart and I hitchhiked to an Ashram for the ceremony. The couple looked stunning and in love, dressed in all white and barefoot. Each wore green leis hanging from their necks and Robin wore a flower wreath around her head. Ann Davies—High Priestess of the Builders of the Adytum Temple (B.O.T.A.)—officiated the intimate ceremony.

Yogi Bhajan, a spiritual teacher who had become a mentor to Jim, was there. Yogi Bhajan was a big influence in Jim's life. Jim and Robin at that time were Sikhs. Jim followed Yogi Bhajan's teachings and became a devoted disciple and later a Master. Only a few were deemed Masters of the Yogi. Robin's mom was there, as was Patrick (Sunflower).

When I first met Yogi Bhajan I was intimidated by his presence. He wore a white turban around his head, he had dark black eyes, and a long black beard. When he stared at me it was like he was looking into my soul. He was surrounded by disciples who seemed devoted to his very being. I could tell Jim and the Yogi had a special bond.

Young Love

Summer 1970

While his mom was away working nights at the Aware Inn, Bart became legendary for throwing parties at his house on Mulholland in the basement he'd converted into a primo hippie hangout, replete with red tapestries, incense, candles, and cozy corners everywhere. In the basement we spent hours on end listening to the Rolling Stones, Led Zeppelin, Crosby, Stills and Nash to name a few. Smoking pot was the thing to do. I could only take one puff and that did it for me. It was a very social time. We always had our group of friends hanging out together.

On weekends Bart would sometimes have a taxi pick me up at my house and take me to International House of Pancakes for breakfast, close to La Cienega Lanes, where we joined the bowling league. On other adventures we went ice skating at Laurel Plaza Ice Capades Chalet. Or sometimes we would go to the movies on Hollywood Boulevard at Grauman's Chinese Theater with our friends. One person would pay, then go to the exit and let everyone else (10 of us) sneak in. Bart also got us into wild (21 & over) shows at the Whisky a Go Go and The Troubadour where he knew (at age 12 1/2) the doormen.

I was so naive about relationships. I had so much to learn—we all did. I had a profound trust in Bart for such a young age. I did almost anything he wanted me to do. We got into all sorts of trouble. Nothing big–just taking the family car out for a joy ride. Hitchhiking all over Hollywood. Sneaking into movie theaters. Having parties at his Laurel Canyon house (they were the place to be). Skinny dipping in the family pool in the middle of the night. Sleeping overnight at his house every weekend. Going to the Love-Ins and concerts in Griffin Park. Hanging out in the hippie scene on Sunset Blvd. Sneaking into Pandora's Box. You know, that sort of thing. We had no supervision and were basically on our own.

Speaking of the Love-Ins—what a scene. Hundreds of people would attend, if not thousands. Bands would be playing, vendors selling food and products appealing to the crowd—incense, pipes, tie-dyed t-shirts. Of course drugs were everywhere. The vibe was amazing—no worries, just love.

It was a time of rebellion. Women didn't wear bras, many didn't wear much of anything. I saw a woman getting harassed by the police for wearing a fishnet top without anything under it. A cop told her to put something on under the top, or else he was going to cite her. She went into the bathroom and painted her breasts. When she came out and pointed her freshly painted pair to the cop saying, "How's this?" He just smiled and walked away. People painted their bodies with brilliant psychedelic patterns— you couldn't tell if they were naked or not.

At one point Bart offered to teach me how to drive. Bart's mom Elaine had a little Aston Martin sports car and Bart, clearly underage, would drive the car all the time. Shortly into our lesson, I somehow crashed the car on Mulholland, smashing the front right end. Fortunately the car was still drivable, and Bart drove us home. Big oops.

On school days, Bart would often come to my school during school hours and look for me. I got nervous. My friends thought it was too much. Some of the boys at school didn't like Bart. I'm not sure why, but maybe they were jealous of him. He was there so often that the teachers thought that he went to school there. When we walked down the street we were the same height, we both had long hair and you couldn't tell who the girl or boy was. I might have been a little taller than him, but Bart wore boots with heels all the time to look taller than me.

Shaking Things Up

Winter 1971

At 6:00 a.m. on February 9, 1971, the San Fernando earthquake shook the LA basin, registering 6.6 on the Richter scale. I was sleeping overnight at my friend Tamara's place—she lived in a tiny apartment behind the Aware Inn—south of it by one store—a little apartment in an alleyway behind Sunset Boulevard. We were sound asleep in one of the bedrooms together when the earthquake hit—suddenly the bed moved from one side of the room to the other. And somehow we slept through it.

Moments later, we woke up to Tamara's mom Mary screaming: "Everyone get up and get out! Earthquake!" Still in our pajamas, we ran out into the alleyway. It was total chaos. Phones everywhere started ringing like crazy. My mom and Bart called me at Tamara's to see if we were ok.

Bart's mom Elaine was particularly traumatized by the disaster and decided to pack up the family and leave town for a while. First they went to Seattle, Washington (Elaine's hometown) for about a month, which was torture for me because I couldn't see Bart. He and his family traveled for a while longer to Vancouver, Victoria, and the San Juan Islands, and then ended up in Big Sur, California, about 300 miles north of Los Angeles on the coast.

One night I was with Tiki at a house party in Laurel Canyon, up Kirkwood, and we were spending the night there. I was telling Tiki how much I missed Bart when she said to me, "Well, why don't we go up to Big Sur and visit him?" Her boyfriend Tom, she said, would accompany us. It sounded like a good plan. Tiki, Tommy, and I would hitchhike from LA to Big Sur to see Bart. The next day, I packed up my backpack with a few belongings, didn't tell anyone what I was doing, and we all headed out on the highway.

How would I find Bart when we arrived in Big Sur? No

problem, I thought about that in advance. In my backpack I brought a black sharpie marker pen. Upon our arrival in Big Sur we located a bend in the road on Highway 1 with a huge white guardrail, clearly visible to anyone who might happen to be driving in the vicinity. Several other people left messages here. It was like a community message board. Tiki and Tommy watched me as I wrote in big bold letters: "Bart—Meet us at Nepenthe today at 3 p.m.—Wendy."

Bart and his family met us at the appointed time and place. However I'm not so sure if Elaine was quite thrilled that the three of us had shown up unannounced, 300 miles away, and broadcast our arrival to everyone in the surrounding community. While I had hoped that we would be welcomed to stay with them, no such invitation was forthcoming. We would be on our own to find a place to sleep for the next few nights. Fortunately, Tiki, Tommy and I met a local musician who invited us—including Bart—to all sleep in the back of a pickup truck.

We all stayed in Big Sur for three days. Bart hung out with us and showed us his favorite places. He took us all on a hike behind Deetjen's Inn in Big Sur. This was Elaine's favorite place to stay. The hike was called "The Seven Dwarfs Trail." I'd never seen anything so magical before. There were seven trees of different sizes and shapes, with hollow openings at the bottoms—with wooden plaques above the openings engraved with the names of each Seven Dwarf.

We followed a path of clovers, some with four leaves, covering the ground alongside a running creek and a waterfall. From a bridge covering the creek, we could see a canopy of redwood trees with big branches draped everywhere. It was a beautiful place and I didn't want to leave.

After the hike we met Elaine and Ben at the Deetjen's restaurant. We were always starving and welcomed a good meal. We stayed for lunch and even met the mean Grandpa who owned Deetjen's, who was legendary in Big Sur. Bart showed us Elaine's room on the bottom floor and his room with Ben upstairs. Most rooms shared bathrooms with other guests. It was a funky and rundown Motel. We also spent time at "The Post Office"—a hippie hangout in the middle of Big Sur.

After three days it was time for all of us to leave. Bart and his family drove back together, and Tiki, Tommy, and I would have to hitchhike back to LA. We had made it about halfway and were thumbing it on the side of the road somewhere near Buttonwillow when a police car pulled up alongside us and an officer looked at Tiki.

"How old are you?"

"18," she lied.

The cops were unconvinced and unamused.

"Today is a school day. Why aren't you guys in school?"

We all awkwardly looked at one another. Totally busted. This was not going well.

Minutes later we were in the back seat of the squad car, en route to Police HQ in Santa Barbara.

Tommy called his mom, who immediately rushed there from LA to pick him up a few hours later. Tiki and I weren't so lucky. When we notified our parents of our predicament, they were less than thrilled with our spontaneous adventure and police entanglements. They were certainly in no hurry to hop in their cars and drive two hours to come and pick us up, and instead seemed to be in *"Let's teach these misbehaving girls a little lesson"*-mode. We would have to stick it out overnight in a holding cell, surrounded by several other underage hitchhikers.

The next morning my mom arrived, accompanied by Bart. When I saw him, I ran up and gave him the biggest hug ever, jumping up and wrapping my arms and legs around him. I was so excited and touched that he made the big trip from LA all the way to see me and make sure that I was OK.

On the car ride home in our 70s Chevy station wagon, Bart had his arm around me the entire time and made me feel so secure and loved. Meanwhile my mom was chain-smoking and yelling at me nonstop. This would prove to be an uncomfortable car ride. I was so mad at my mom for making us stay there all night, and she was equally furious at me for getting into all kinds of trouble and making her have to drive out to the middle of nowhere.

After this little episode, I think Elaine may have been a bit put off by the intensity of our relationship, and things were different after everyone returned from Big Sur to LA. Bart and I stayed together a bit longer, but there was strain in the air. We started fighting a lot. We were so young and our relationship was too intense. We didn't know how to handle the love we had. In my mind, I was becoming more interested in spirituality, while Bart was continuing his partying lifestyle. A few weeks later, as Bart and I were in his mom's bedroom sitting by the fireplace, I looked at him and said, "It's over." And he said, "It's ok." Too much too soon.

Wendy (me) and Bart (both age 12)
having dinner at The Aware Inn

Chapter 2

THE MOTHER HOUSE

Hitchin'

Spring 1971

Despite the setbacks, our hitchhiking trip to Big Sur emboldened Tiki and I to set our sights on other potential destinations. We learned about an upcoming "Sit In" in San Francisco's Golden Gate Park as a peaceful protest against the Vietnam War. San Francisco was easily five or six hours away.

Too far for us to go? Nope. Tiki, Tommy, and I made it to the Haight Ashbury in one single trip, when we got picked up by a van in LA that was also headed to the Sit In. People of all ages, from teenagers on up, were there. Many were giving out free food in the park. There were girls wearing shirts with no bras, flashing peace signs—the smell of incense wafting from windows—thousands of people sitting in the streets—people having sex in the park—peace and love, not war—musicians on the sidewalks playing electrifying acid rock—and let's be honest, lots of drugs—although I didn't partake.

However, on the way back from San Francisco to Los Angeles, we encountered some difficulties. One guy who had picked us up started acting suspicious. Tommy was sitting up front, and Tiki and I were in the back seat. Tommy turned back and looked back at us, and we all knew what to do. We held our fingers on the electric door locks, so that the driver wouldn't be able to lock us in.

Without warning, the driver suddenly veered his car off the road and turned into an abandoned cornfield. He provided no explanation and showed no signs of stopping. This was bad. Tiki, Tommy, and I all looked at each other again, nodded, then banged open the passenger doors and leapt out of the moving vehicle into the cornfield. The car kept going, leaving us stranded and walking a mile back to the main highway. Somehow we finally made it back to LA, and strangely this didn't deter us in the least.

Hitchhiking adventures with Tiki and others continued, and over the course of time I was picked up for rides by some of the biggest musicians in the Laurel Canyon crew—David Crosby, Graham Nash, Neil Young, James Taylor, Bob Dylan, and Donovan, to name a few.

One time on Santa Monica Boulevard in West Hollywood outside Shakey's Pizza with my girlfriends Thea, Terri, and Susan (aka Snot), we were picked up by none other than Elvis Presley. My friends made me sit next to him. However, by this time, this was no longer the young, sexy Elvis we remembered. He'd put on a few pounds and was perspiring profusely. When he invited us up to his hotel in Beverly Hills, we let him know that we were age 14. He kindly delivered us to the doorstep of our girlfriend's Thea's house in Sunset Plaza and let us ramble on.

Rock 'n' Roll High School

Summer 1971

By this time I met a new boy at Fairfax High School named Ronnie. He was two years older than me and was friends with my oldest sister. Ronnie was in a band with four other guys. He was the lead guitarist and could play almost any instrument—he was beyond talented. I spent most of my time with Ronnie and his band. He was my next intense relationship.

Ronnie taught me a lot about music. I was not musically inclined. I was unaware of anyone like that who could play piano, guitar, bass, and could sing. He was so passionate and focused on his craft. He told me that he used to play the guitar in front of huge audiences when he was in elementary school. He was born talented. A prodigy. I used to go over to his house after school and hang out in his living room and watch him beautifully play the piano. I would sit next to him on the bench and he would play gorgeous classical music. I was in awe of how he moved his fingers flawlessly.

In another room he had his electric guitar. He put my fingers on the fretboard and said, "Try this chord, try that chord." He had a portable amplifier in his room. The sound was loud and huge. I went to every single practice he had with his band. They would practice 5-6 hours in the evening and with an audience of the girlfriends of the band guys. Michael played rhythm guitar. Sean was the drummer. John on bass. They all sang and they were all amazing. They played in all the school performances.

Years later, I heard that Ronnie later became a studio musician. I knew he could play every instrument, so it made sense that bands would hire him to do backup. He knew every rock n roll song. Every folk song. I heard that he later traveled with the Red Hot Chili Peppers as a backup musician.

Ronnie and I went to concerts every Saturday night. That was our life together. It was amazing. It was a fun relationship, but it wasn't going to do it for me—it wasn't going to sustain me. I was looking for something different—and I had to figure out what that was. I didn't stay in the relationship with Ronnie because I was drawn to the spiritual world.

After Ronnie and I broke up, during the Summer of 1971 I worked at the Hollywood Bowl as an usher in the box seats. Yes I was underage (barely 14), and I might have forged my mom's name to get a work permit. In retrospect, it was the right decision. That was an incredible summer. Virtually everyone in the audience was taking acid and smoking pot. I had the best seats in the house to see so many of the greats—Jethro Tull, Donovan, Joni Mitchell.

Sometimes this included attending the after parties, surrounded by celebrities. One time, Led Zeppelin guitarist Jimmy Page was hitting on me backstage at The Forum, and kept commenting on the size of my lips. I was so embarrassed and nervous. What was about to happen? At last, he looked a little closer at me and said, "You're not 16 you're 12!" He was off by a couple years, but close enough. Needless to say (or is it?) nothing happened.

Towards the end of the summer, I went to see the Grateful Dead at the Hollywood Palladium with my sister Marcia and two other childhood friends—Michelle and Nancy—who had grown up with me in our neighborhood. They were already working at The Source and partaking in meditation classes with Jim Baker.

Amidst the colorful crowd, my friends were the only ones in the audience wearing all white.

We all got to go backstage and meet people and all the band crew. It was at this show I met Marcia's new boyfriend Roy, and his friends James and Bobby. The three boys worked for a concert company—James did lighting and Bobby set up the stage for concert tours.

I was taken by James instantly. He looked Jesus-like. He had green eyes, long golden brown hair, a beard and mustache, and his teeth were a little bucked. He was kind and loving. Always complimenting me. Which is something I wasn't used to. He was funny—always cracking me up—and very sociable. Easy to talk to and playful. Meanwhile, I was quiet, shy, and insecure. Opposites attracted. He originally came from Chicago and was ditching the draft because he didn't believe in the Vietnam War, like so many men his age.

The Last Straw

Fall 1971

Between all the hitchhiking and cutting class, I managed to get kicked out of Fairfax High a couple times and do some memorable stints at Beverly Hills High School and Hollywood High. By the Fall of 1971 I was back at Fairfax High beginning the 10th grade. It was no picnic. State-mandated busing programs were forcing integration of students from vastly different ethnic and socio-economic backgrounds, sometimes with unintended volatile results. There was a lottery—and if they pulled your name, you would either stay at Fairfax High School, or be bussed to Los Angeles High School. I got to stay at Fairfax—lucky me.

The students from LA High School were largely uncomfortable being at Fairfax High, and many were acting up in the classroom. From my perspective, there was no support network to make this a smooth transition. To my knowledge, there was no counseling, no security, no preparation. It just seemed like a mess and out of control. The teachers seemed helpless. Frustrating for everyone—the kids who had to come to Fairfax, against their will, and those of us who stayed, and had our world turned upside down into a huge mish-mosh.

The last straw came a few months into 10th grade. I was in the bathroom minding my own business when I was attacked by four girls who were bussed in through the integration program from Los Angeles High School. They pulled my hair, threw me down, and stomped on my stomach, twisting my leg. I was in complete shock and was laying on the floor huddled in a ball when another girl found me there and alerted the Principal. I was bleeding and my head was cut.

The Principal called my mom when she was at work. My mom refused to come to school and pick me up, and she told the nurse that I should just take the bus home. Unfortunately I had used my four dimes to buy lunch, so I didn't have enough money for the bus, and had to walk home in complete shambles from Fairfax High School to La Cienega, along Melrose Avenue. I walked past art shops and restaurants, my hair disheveled and blood dripping down my face, cheeks bruised and swollen. When I arrived home, no one was there, so I went up to my room by myself and I cried, thinking, "This cannot be my life."

The situation was so bad that I started cutting school. A lot. I had mom's signature down pat for getting out of class. I loved school and learning, but there was chaos in the classroom and I felt like public education had failed me. I begged my Mom to take me out of the school, but Mom said no. Later, when my Mom went to meet with the Principal, she told her: "Wendy ditches too much." True enough. I was so over it. I wanted out.

When Mom wouldn't let me go to a different school, I asked my Counselor if I could take the G.E.D.—the General Educational Development Test. It consisted of four basic topics: Math, Critical Thinking, Science, and Social Studies. The deal was, if you passed it, you would get a GED diploma. And legally, I wouldn't have to return to high school.

In order to take the G.E.D. you needed to get a signed permission from your parents. In my case, I had mastered my mother's signature and could write it even better than she could. So my mom had no idea I was taking the test. I studied my brains out with my friends Jodie and Julie. All three of us passed the test.

The New Path

Spring 1972

I had to make some changes in my life. I decided to follow a different path. I knew my sister Marcia was involved with a morning meditation class that Jim Baker was leading. I was intrigued by the change in my sister—she was much calmer and seemed happier. At this time my sister Marcia practically moved out and lived with some of her new friends from "The Source Restaurant." And

I thought to myself, "Maybe this is a path that I should explore to make some changes?"

I decided to go with my sister Marcia to a meditation class on the corner of Robertson and Melrose in the heart of West Hollywood. The class took place in the back of an antique store owned by Jules Buccieri, who was friends with Bart's dad. Before you walk into the class, you have to take off your shoes. And then, you have to find a place to sit, on the floor, and wait for the spiritual leader to guide us in meditation. Unbeknownst to me, our leader that day was Jim. He immediately recognized me, and gave me a wink. Right away, my mind was full of questions and trying to figure out what it was all about.

The first thing that we had to do was sit cross-legged in a full or half lotus position, and our hands had to be above our knees, with the palms facing up. We started to do a chant. And I had to learn this chant—*Nam Myo Ho Renge Kyo*. We chanted this for at least 30 minutes, which seemed to put us in a state of bliss. After this chant, we started doing Hatha yoga breathing exercises. With controlled breathing, you could get away from the physical being and to elevate into a higher being. There were a lot of inhales—holding it in for long periods of time, and then exhaling—repetitiously over a period of several minutes. Then you could go to the next level of meditation.

At this point, my legs were in excruciating pain from sitting so long. But the leader of the chant said that if you do the breathing exercises, you can transmute your pain into pleasure. This intrigued me and surprised me—how much I was affected by this exercise.

At the end of the one hour meditation class, I was so high on my breath. I never felt so light and pure. And this was my first introduction to a new spiritual path. Now I understood why my sister was so happy and was doing so well—in an environment that was loving and kind with positive energy flowing every-where—quite the opposite from our life at home. It seemed to give her a sense of belonging. Knowing this was Bart's father, Jim, leading the meditation made me feel more comfortable. Even though I hadn't seen Bart for a while, we still had that special bond.

Soon I began spending a lot less time at school and a lot more time at The Source Restaurant. After school on most afternoons I started working at The Source Restaurant as a juicer. My older sister Marcia preceded me in this role, and helped me to get hired, when she got promoted to become a waitress. My job was unpaid, but I didn't care—I just wanted to be there. My mom either didn't notice or care that Marcia wasn't living at home any-more. But I noticed and was confused as to why my mom never said anything.

By this time, the three boys I met at the Grateful Dead show—Roy, James, and Bobby—had all started working at The Source, during a hiatus in their concert crew jobs. They also started to participate in the meditation classes, eating all vege-tarian foods, and hanging out with Jim Baker. My sister, and our good friends Nancy and Michelle, started seriously working at The Source. Bobby (Damian) became the manager. Roy (Pyth-ias) worked in the kitchen.

James (aka Ramacharaka) worked at The Source with me, doing prep for the juicing. We started to have a friendship, which later turned into a romantic relationship. I was completely falling for him and I enjoyed being with him as much as possible. Ram-acharaka would pick me up at my house in one of the Source vans and bring me to the restaurant.

I loved working there. All the juices were freshly squeezed. My favorite drink was Apple, Beet, Pineapple juice—very popular and healthy. After years of growing up with such an unhealthy diet, this was a refreshing change. I could feel a physical difference in my mind and body.

Within a few months, I became a waitress and worked the night shift. At the time, I was still in school, so I was getting very little sleep. At night my feet were vibrating—I was so tired and sleep deprived. As a waitress, I waited on lots of celebrities. One who stood out was Goldie Hawn. Goldie was young, beautiful and spirited. She was so nice and easy-going.

I also waited on Cher, who came into the restaurant all the time with Sonny Bono. Cher was always sweet. Cher had a girlfriend there with her and they were talking about her relationship. While I didn't wait on John Lennon, other people did. He came in with Yoko and Paul McCartney. He came in mostly at night when I wasn't working. Many of these celebrities frequented The Aware Inn and already knew Jim from his days there.

Lots of famous bands visited The Source, as it became a celebrity magnet in the middle of the Sunset Strip. We were known for our vegetarian cuisine, and for beautiful women with long flowing hair. Jim Baker was a big attraction. He knew a lot of these people. It was a cool place to be. It was unique—there was nothing else like it. People were interested and intrigued by what we were doing as a community at The Source.

Family Beginnings (#36)

One day, after a meditation with Yogi Bhajan, (Jim's master and mentor in the Sikh religion), Jim Baker was talking with his wife Robin and Patrick, a young guy they met at Yogi Bhajan's ashram. Patrick said to Jim Baker, "We should open up a church in the Source parking lot on Sundays—open to the public."

Jim responded, "You know, you're right."

Patrick was given the name Sunflower by Jim Baker, and Sunflower became the #1 member in the new Family.

And just like that, The Source Family began. This is how the story was told in the commune. Jim decided that anyone who joined the newly-founded "Brotherhood of the Source Family" would be given a new name (by Jim) and a number, denoting the order in which they committed to being part of the Family. This is when Jim became known as Father.

Sunflower built The Temple in the back of the parking lot of The Source—which could fit up to 20 people. The Temple was all made out of wood, and no nails were used in the construction—a real testament to Sunflower's craftsmanship. This is where Father started teaching for his new church, including morning meditations.

Many Family members were living in the West Hollywood area in different locations. Some of us were living at home. Others were living in apartments. Jim and Robin (who became Ahom, aka Mother) were living upstairs, above The Source Restaurant.

Father wanted us all to live together as a true family—and start his new way of life. We began a hunt for a house to live with all the new people who had joined. By early Springtime,

The Family was growing in numbers and collectively embarked on an experiment in communal living at The Mother House. The Chandler Mansion, at 2411 Inverness Avenue in Los Feliz, would become our new homebase.

In March 1972 scores of Family Members started moving into The Mother House. This included my sister Marcia, who officially joined The Family and was given the name Mate. While I was still living at home with my mom and sisters, I started spending more and more time with The Family. One morning, during meditation, Father gave me the new name—Lila. It wasn't long before the fateful night when I decided to leave home to go to morning meditation at the Mother House, and I never returned. Right at that moment, barely 15 years old, I decided that I was all in. I became Family Member #36.

Me at age 15 at The Source Restaurant
(credit: Isis Aquarian)

The Mother House was three stories high, and there was a guesthouse and a maid's quarters. We had a pool by the front yard entrance. There was a green lawn in a circle around the driveway. I lived on the third story at first, then I lived on the bottom level by the kitchen (maid's quarters). Later I lived above the garage in the guesthouse.

The garage was converted into the herb lab, where Bo (the herb guy) would make herb supplements and medicine. We also had a loom to embroider belts, and a leather section to make sandals and belts. Boaz, a family member, taught us all how to make moccasins and belts. We were very crafty and artistic. Sunflower made jewelry for us all—he made me a Starman medallion necklace, which I have to this day. I loved the Mother House. We shared so many magical moments.

At the Mother House we would all take these long walks in the neighborhood. Imagine fifty people dressed in white robes and dresses, all with flowing hair, men with beards, and all so vibrant and healthy, walking by your neighborhood. We attracted a lot of attention. We all surrounded Father and paid close heed to whatever he was saying. It was always so far out to hear his visions of life and esoteric messages. I wanted to learn as much as possible. I hung on to his every word. I wanted to be a perfect disciple.

Morning meditations were the most angelic and beautiful experiences. At 4:00 a.m. the Family members would gather their spots on the carpet in the living room at the Mother House. I would place a blanket folded up to sit on. I made a place for Ramacharaka and me. By this time, he and I were a couple.

Ramacharaka would sit down and start meditating. I would

prepare his coffee and bring it to him. Making coffee was an art. First the boiling water goes into the mug (to make the mug hot), then the coffee, then I pour hot half and half into the coffee, then I put in a spoonful of warm honey, mixing it all together. It was like candy coffee. We both would sit down and drink our coffee, and wait for morning meditation to start. Sometimes if I was early getting organized I would brush Ramacharaka's long hair.

One of Father's Ten Commandments was: "The man and his woman are one, let nothing separate them." Father taught us his philosophy on how the woman serves her man, and in return he provides for her. This teaching resonated with me. I use this in my relationship today. To me it meant to always support your man's confidence and take care of all his physical needs. Make your man a king in his world. The Source Family relationship commitment was a huge attraction for me.

Once enough Family members were sitting down in full lotus position, the chanting would just start. It sounded like angels singing from heaven. We had all these different chants. There was always a leader guiding us along. We chanted "AHOM" a lot. It sounded like music and instruments flowing from our mouths.

We had morning meditations everyday religiously. We all waited for Father to come and lead morning meditation. Once Father arrived we all chanted some more, and did Hatha yoga and breathing exercises. After that Father would give us a sermon about anything that came to him. Father said he was channeling the Akashic Records from his angels and guides. It was always a mind blowing experience.

The things that came out of Father's mouth were so heavy. "The only constant thing in life is change." *Sheeeeew!* (this was an exclamation we used to express being in awe) Consequently we were constantly changing. He spoke esoterically, but for some reason, I understood everything. He had a rare gift of explaining his thought process. It was always so inspiring and we couldn't wait to get started.

A typical class would last at least two hours, not including chanting to Omne (which means "the sun") at sunrise, while doing the Star Exercise. For this exercise (often performed at sunrise and sunset), you would stand barefoot with your legs a few feet apart, with arms outstretched, so your body takes the shape of a star. You hold your left palm up and right palm down, and breathe intensely.

After morning meditation we would clean up our spaces and everyone would get on with their jobs. Some went to work at the restaurant and others had responsibilities in the house. Sometimes Father would hang out at the house and talk some more with the few members that could. At times some would go swimming and do exercises in the pool. Most women walked around topless and only wore their skirts. This wasn't unusual at all.

I was only 15 and I had never shown my breasts to anybody other than my mirror. At first, I was humiliated to take my shirt off because everyone had breasts except me. It didn't happen overnight, but eventually I felt a sense of vigor and freedom— and tore my top off. It was exhilarating. At my age, I was lucky to have anything. Initially it felt a little weird. But after a while, it was fine because everyone was doing it.

My time at the Mother House was my favorite. It was the first time I felt happiness and love. Anyone in The Family was now my mentor and role model. I loved watching the Mothers treat their children with so much love and kindness. Some of the Mothers were still breastfeeding and I had never seen this before. My new sisters were so kind to me. This was definitely a new experience for me.

I found myself dancing around the house with excitement. I would often sing along to the music playing, whether it be live from Ahom and Aladdin or on stereo in the house. Music was always playing during the day. My favorite song was *Friends* by Elton John and any Moody Blues music. My new sisters were my teachers. They constantly reminded me of Father's philosophy—like: don't have an ego, love one another, commit to the practice, be at one with the universe, treat your temple (body) with respect, and so on.

When I first joined the commune I had to abide by all the rules. Rule number 1 is to be a vegetarian. Rule number 2: Never cut your hair. Rule number 3: Eat only two meals a day. Rule number 4: Wake up every morning at 4:00 a.m. and get ready for meditation class at 4:30 a.m. Rule number 5: Take a cold shower upon waking up. Rule number 6: Commit to the disciplines given by Father. Rule number 7: Don't watch television, listen to radio, or read newspapers. These were a few of our basic rules. However many more rules were added on as time went by.

I always felt like I was learning something new. Each day when I woke up I felt challenged and excited to learn. I was soaking in all the spoken wisdom around me—whether it be by Father or the Family members. I realized that I lived in a bubble and only thought a certain way. Being at the Mother House full-time gave me the opportunity to grow spiritually. If I had stayed at home, I don't feel I would have had the same ultimate experience.

I thanked God everyday that I got to live there. This was exactly what I was looking for. Pure Mother House bliss everyday. My favorite time was when Father would come to visit and hang out with us. I enjoyed hearing him talk about life and spirituality. I was a sponge in my Spiritual High School, constantly learning.

Sunday Meals at The Source

Sunday meals at The Source were the best of all. The women did all the preparations, while the men sat in front of Father, who would be giving a sermon of some sort. We made salad in big wooden bowls with lots of vegetables. A typical meal was Romaine lettuce, bell peppers, tomatoes, alfalfa sprouts, walnuts, avocados, bean sprouts, mushrooms, beets, carrots, cheese grated and cucumbers.

We always made our own dressing. The dressing was different every time. Sometimes it was creamy with avocados, sour cream, lemon and herbs. Other times it was apple cider vinegar, lemon, garlic and mustard. Always homemade. We cut up fruit and put it on platters. We had fresh homemade bread and butter. And of course a special dessert.

Our meals were legendary—not only for the feast, but the display and company. The men set up long tables with chairs. We all sat together and blessed our food before anyone ate. Music would be playing and sounds of laughter. This was the beginning of The Family. After our meal was over, typically Robin (aka Ahom) and Tim (aka Aladdin) would play the guitar and sing their own songs. Members would dance to their music and some would sing along. A euphoric world. We all would clean up and make it spotless for the next day's Source Restaurant opening.

We would all pile into the blue and white vans and head home to our Los Feliz Mother House. We went to bed early, meditated at night to get up early the next morning for meditation classes. The house was always quiet after dark. Early to bed, early to rise.

Early days—Morning meditation at
The Source (in the parking lot)

The Mystic Road

Spring 1972

Soon after I moved into The Mother House full-time, I received a book produced and written by Father Yod (Jim Baker) called *The Mystic Road*—a series of mental and physical exercises intended to enhance your powers of concentration, enable your ability to use the 'Universal Life Energy', and develop your nerve center, or plexuses of power.

The goal was to open up the chakras—and get rid of the negativity in your thoughts to turn it into positive thinking. In its opening pages, it read: "You think with your mind. In other words, it is your servant, the instrument which the real 'you' uses to manifest. The purpose now is to bring the mind under the complete control of the real you." It was an intense, disciplined thought process. This exercise gave me that powerful gift. I have used these techniques throughout my life.

This exercise took 12 weeks to finish. The program was done daily. Each week was a different exercise. It began with 10 minutes per night, and gradually increased—by the twelfth week, each exercise lasted up to an hour. There was a method to it.

The Mystic Road became a prerequisite initiation for any new members who wanted to join The Family. I diligently practiced each stage of The Mystic Road, meditating in the lotus position on a sheepskin rug in front of an altar with a pyramid-shaped mirror, lighting a candle and burning incense. As I progressed through the journey I developed the ability to close my eyes and immediately go into a deep meditation space.

Several times while meditating, I had out-of-body experiences where I felt like I was levitating above the room. I wondered to myself, "Should I go back down to Earth, or should I stay up here in the Heavens?" When I later related my experiences to other Family members, I found out that others also had similar episodes.

I levitated—floating up and looking down at myself. Feeling light as air. Out of body. In the 'now' moment. Completely free of all bodily functions. Not of the body. Like my being was out and I had no control of my functions. And the physical body was down there. And I had a choice to make. At the time, it felt right and it felt good. Then all of a sudden it hit me that I needed to go back to earth to my earthly spiritual body. At that minute, my mind said: "Go back to Earth."

It was unbelievable. I was meditating, and in the lotus position, could feel my body still on the ground, but my spiritual self rising up. I was looking down at my physical body. This is crazy. This is outrageous—an orgasmic, light feeling. Then I would make the decision to go back, slip into my body, open my eyes, and see myself in the mirror. I had this experience many times. I could never have the experience knowingly—I only had the experience unexpectedly. It was not up to me, it was up to a higher source.

One time, I was all alone at The Mother House on the third floor, meditating by myself and I began Exercise 10 of The Mystic Road. I opened my eyes and looked into the mirror, where I was shocked to see, as clear as day, an old Indian medicine woman with wrinkly skin and long gray braids. All around her was light. She looked wise and amazing. Full of confidence. Strong. Everything that I wasn't at that time.

She wore jewelry of turquoise, silver, and feathers—symbols I later learned showed that she was a medicine woman. The collar of her top was all jewelry and feathers. She had a beaded head-band with feathers coming down on the side.

Most strikingly, she had my same eyes. It was like I was look-ing at another version of myself in the mirror. It was like looking into myself from a past life—with my eyes. Was this me? Was I looking at myself?

I couldn't handle this and I was so scared. I leapt up and ran around the house screaming. It was strange to be all alone there in the late afternoon. What could it mean?

When Father returned, I told him about my vision. I said that I wasn't ready for this. He smiled and said, "Yes, Daughter, Child, you were an Indian medicine woman in your past life. This wouldn't have happened to you unless you were ready."

It affected me to the point that it gave me some confidence. The Mystic Road was about developing your inner confidence and strengths. This exercise became my school. I studied hard and tried to perfect this practice. I was only fifteen years old at the time. The Mystic Road lasted for twelve weeks and I ended up doing this exercise two times.

In a White Robe

We started off wearing only white clothing. The women wore only dresses or skirts with blouses. The length was always long or close to it. The women decorated their outfits with turquoise jewelry and silver belts. Birkenstocks or sandals were the pref-erence of shoes—or barefoot. We bought our clothing at either

"The Rose Bowl swap meets" or Olvera Street in downtown
Los Angeles. The stores there were full of white clothing and
embroidering. The men wore white light cotton pants with
white shirts. We also wore turbans around our heads, because
we were following the Sikh religion. This was called the Essene
Headdress.

Our styles evolved over time. Later on, we started sewing
our own clothes. We made white dresses and shawls with white
homespun materials. Men initially wore pants—then later we
made the men robes, with a sash across the waist. All clothes
were sewn by hand or sewing machine by the women. After that
we went into velvet and materials with color. We made all of
our own clothes, all of our own shawls, and moccasins, and we
learned how to make belts from a loom.

The Cleanse

Summer 1972

While The Mystic Road was a mental exercise, aimed at achiev-
ing purity of thought, the Yod He Vah He diet was intended to
physically cleanse the body. Everyone who joined The Family did
the Yod He Vah He diet—also called The Rainbow Diet—like
an initiation. Its purpose was to cleanse your mind and body,
to get ready for what's to come—to clean you out, spiritually,
mentally, emotionally, physically.

The Yod He Vah He diet consisted of foods from all the different colors of the rainbow—avocado, alfalfa sprouts, banana, 1
small eggplant, 1 cup filbert's nuts, 1 large tomato, 1 quarter red

onion, two cloves of garlic. Mix and match any way you choose. (pg. 40 of The Source Restaurant Recipes). If you could do the diet for 30 days, then you were ready to commit to being one of Father's disciples. This diet was not an easy task. But everyone who wanted to join The Family had to complete this diet. Then they were allowed to take the next step.

After completing The Mystic Road and the Yod He Va He diet, Father told me, "You still have too many poisons in your body. You need to go on a grape juice fast now." (Father learned about the grape juice fast from Professor Szekely at Rancho la Puerta in Tecate, Mexico—I found out much later on while visiting The Museum at Rancho). I was now moved above the guesthouse. I shared a room with Amber and Makushla. Makushla wasn't with Father yet as his woman.

I began a grape juice fast—this 30-day fast was intended to cleanse the system and purify the body. During the cleanse I started eliminating, a lot—which is another way of saying that I was getting sick. Father told me that I had lots of poisons in my body, likely a result from years of eating TV dinners and drinking formula as a baby, as opposed to nursing.

I was not nursed as a baby. My mother's education was to feed her babies formula—processed milk with sugar added. I later learned that it is not healthy for the baby and doesn't give the baby the proper start of life, as comes from mother's milk. The first two weeks after the baby is born, the "milk" is colostrum, which is essential to put fat on the baby, giving them the nutrition that they need to fight infection and disease. Nursing gives the baby a better chance of being strong and healthy. It's good for the mom to nurse the baby, and helps the abdomen to contract to its original size. It is also a bonding experience between baby and mother—full of vitamins and nutrients—the way nature intended.

Father said there is so much cancer in the world—and it was his belief that you should nurse your baby for three years—until the baby no longer wants it—two years, as the baby wants it (on demand)—and for the third year, maybe nurse at night or in the morning—gradually weaning them off.

As I began the fast, I noticed a small boil developing under my left arm, near my lymph nodes. At first it was small, and I carried on, not paying much attention to it. However, as days went by, the boil grew bigger and bigger. I started feeling sick, like I had the flu (in The Family we called this "elimination")—and within a week I was mostly bedridden, with Makushla, Soma, and Amber taking care of me. Ramacharaka and my sister would visit me, and Father would periodically come and check in on me.

Our herb guy Bo made an herbal paste of echinacea and goldenseal to draw out the poisons. He placed the pack under my arm daily. The boil continued to grow and was sensitive to the touch. Every day Father would look at it and examine it. I started feeling delirious and out of it.

Father had vast medical knowledge, having studied with Dr. Walters—the Baker family physician who had a holistic, natural way of healing the body—and others to learn about holistic health.

Father told me, "If you went to Western doctors, they would diagnose you with lymphoma cancer." He said to be patient, because "You can't do anything until there are three heads on the boil." He didn't know how long that would take. It ended up taking over a month to happen.

As my arm grew huge, I had to keep it elevated. After about a month and a half, I had this big purple boil festering on my arm, and I started to get a high fever, which would persist for several weeks. It grew to be about the size of an orange, totally nasty.

I probably should have been hospitalized, but I was completely devoted to Father, and believed in him and his philosophy of healing. I believed that he knew what he was doing, and I put my life in his hands. I felt I was doing the right thing. I never was scared—I trusted him so much. I never thought about going to a doctor or a hospital, even though I was delirious from the fever.

At last, the time came. Father told me, "Ok, we are ready, Child. You have three heads now. Tomorrow morning I will have you brought to The Source Restaurant upstairs to my room. And we're gonna release the poison from your body."

Finally—I couldn't wait to get these poisons out of my body.

He told me that he was going to take a glass bottle to sterilize—putting it in boiling hot water. Then he would cover my arm with a cloth, and then use the bottle to put intense pressure on the boil, to extract the toxins. At the time, the boil was so painful, I couldn't even touch it. The three heads meant that all the poisons were ready—(wait until 3 heads)—Father Yod said, "Everything comes in threes."

What could I say? I was like: "I'm ready, let's do it."

Early the next morning, I was carried out of the Mother House into a minivan. I must have weighed barely 90 pounds at this point. I was dizzy and didn't remember the drive to The Source or how I got up the ladder to go into Father's room. I was laid down on white pillows and sheets in the middle of the floor. Next to me, a portable camping stove with boiling water.

There to support me were Ramacharaka, Pythias, Damian, Sunflower, Ahom, Makushla, and Amber. Several of the women took turns putting hot compresses of goldenseal and herbs onto the boil. Meanwhile, Bo "the herb guy" downstairs made the pastes, which would be used to heal the skin.

First, we all smoked the sacred herb to get relaxed and calm. Everybody was calm. I was starting to get scared at this point.

Father began preparing the area on my arm. He told me, "We are going to release the poisons. All the impurities from your childhood and cancers are going to come out."

I meekly responded, "OK."

I laid down, arms outstretched, naked, totally trusting the process. I thought that either I was going to die, or live to tell the tale. Or it won't work—and I'll live the rest of my life with the giant boil.

Everyone started chanting. Between the fever, the herb, the predicament, seeing the bottle there and all the towels, looking into Father's eyes and sensing his energy—I felt like I was in the middle of a surreal movie.

Father said, "Everyone has to hold her down. She can't move."

Father took a hot bottle out of the boiling water. He held it up high, and then brought it down fast onto the boil. Boom! A flood torrent of pus, blood, and water came streaming out of my arm. Father kept pressing down, running his fingers up and down my arm, squeezing out more and more toxins. It was like a waterfall pouring out of my arm.

Father explained to the others gathered in the room, "She

is getting rid of old impurities—getting rid of her old life."
Reaction from the room: "Shewwww . . . Far out . . ." (Shew was a
vocalized reaction to hearing a heavy situation—it was a sigh that
we often expressed after a profound, awe-inspiring statement from
Father. Along the lines of "oooh" and "awww"—but more intense.
It was part of our own language. We would also say things like, "Far
out heavy"—another part of our language.)

The entire time, I was wide awake, with no painkillers.
While it was happening, I felt like I was dying a death, and being
reborn. I could see a white light everywhere, and felt like I was
leaving my body. I was seeing stars. There was a massive hole in
my arm . . . poisons erupting like a fountain. I thought, "So this
is what it's like when you die."

When the ordeal was over at last, I was shaking and had the
chills. I was crying. I couldn't believe that I was still alive. I was
so happy that it was over. Almost immediately, I felt really good.
Even lighter. I was lying there for the next half hour as everyone
cleaned up. Amber was massaging my feet, Ahom was petting
my hair, being motherly, saying that everything would be alright.

Father said to me, "Let's see if you could sit up." There was
still drainage coming out, but it was ok. I sat up and wrapped a
towel around the huge hole in my arm.

I turned to Father and said, "That was such a heavy experience." Then I told him about seeing the white lights.

Father said, "Yes, my Child, you have been reborn. You are
purified. This has cleansed you. All the TV dinners that mom
fed you have left your body." With my rebirth came a new name.
Father told me, in front of all who were gathered, "We will now
call you *Nirvana*."

Father then began a sermon, teaching us all about the process of elimination. He always used any opportunity of something that happened, as a teaching experience. It was analyzed and talked about—broken up—for all to understand.

Father asked me, "How do you feel, my Child? What do you want to do now?"

I told him that I wanted to go onto the Kundalini bar and hang upside down. This was a gravity bar, behind the Temple, where you would pull your legs up over the bar and wrap your feet around the rope that's attached to each side of the bar. I would drop my hands and head, hanging upside down, in order to release kundalini energy—which feels like an intense surge of force flowing from the base of your spine, releasing through the top of your brain.

I went outside with Ramacharaka and Pythias, and I started hanging upside down. You hang upside down there with your upper thigh against the bars—two pads, with one for each leg.

When I got off the bar, Father again asked me, "How do you feel?"

"I feel like a different person."

I felt light and rejuvenated and had a different perspective on the way that I looked at things. Now I was even more-so a devoted believer. Soon I started to learn and appreciate how your diet affects the way you think and feel. I was more clear and attentive in meditations and in belief. I became more committed to being vegetarian—organic and healthy—as a pure way to live. And sugar was an evil in the body, to be avoided. I truly felt reborn.

"Happiness and laughter are part of
a good elimination program.
People need it along with love, peace,
and harmony."
—*The Source Recipe Book*

Father Yod leads Sunday Morning Meditation Class
in the parking lot of The Source Restaurant
Me to the right of Father Yod,
in the second row from the top

Chapter 3

IDLE IN THE WILD

Hauled Into Court

Fall 1972

Weeks later I was working at The Source Restaurant when a police officer showed up and served a summons to someone who was working there. It was a message to be delivered to me—but I didn't know what the papers meant. We went upstairs and showed the papers to Father, and he reviewed them. He told me that I would have to appear in court in two weeks to face my mother, who had reported me for running away from home.

Father made me feel like everything was going to be fine, saying, "Don't worry, they are not going to take you away."

He told me that he would send me to court with representation. Family member Magus was older and a psychologist, and Father thought that he would be the best person in The Family to represent me.

Over the next two weeks, I was enjoying every moment at The Mother House that I possibly could. I was in constant fear of having to go back home. After living in the beautiful loving environment, the thought of going back to a dreary, unhealthy, unloving life scared me. I had total faith in Father that this would not happen, and I prayed every day that I would get to stay and live my life in The Source Family. I could never imagine what was about to happen.

It was strange that my sister Marcia was not also being taken to court. Why was I being singled out? Marcia, who was also living at The Mother House, was never a part of this court proceeding. I was trying to process why I was the only one in The Family who was being taken to court. Other underage Family members were also having issues with their families. And some of them had to leave and go back home. Others were able to convince their parents to let them stay.

I was the happiest I had ever been while living in The Mother House. When the court date arrived, I kissed Ramacharaka goodbye and headed downtown with Magus.

We arrived at 8:00 a.m. in court that day in downtown LA. We had to wait out in the hallway with all of the other cases waiting to be heard. Magus wrote our names down and we were at the bottom of the case loads. I saw my mother walk inside the hallway with her attorney. She didn't look at me or talk to me. I was thankful for this because I had no desire to see her or talk to her. My thoughts were that we would go inside and tell the judge my story about my homelife and then we would go back to the Family while waiting for a verdict. We waited until 3:00 p.m. to go inside the room.

We arrived at court and it wasn't the typical courtroom that you might visualize from TV. It was a small, eerie, dark, plain, windowless room with simple tables and chairs—intimate, foreboding, and not what I expected. The female judge presided from a slightly elevated podium wearing a gown, with two police bailiffs standing on either side, along with a social worker and a court stenographer.

I was wearing all white—a skirt and a blouse. Magus wore white pants, a shirt, and a white turban. He seemed to know how to handle the court system. My mom was sitting on one side at a table with her legal counsel. I sat on another side with Magus.

The minute I walked in, I was in a different place. I turned into a scared little girl. This was the first time I had seen my mom in months. And in the meantime, I had been through so much cleansing. I must have looked different to my mom, because I felt so different. To me, she looked angry and sad, and confident about why we were there. And I soon became not so confident, and concerned about the outcome.

I was shy and had no clue what was going on. I'd never been in trouble like this before. It was totally surreal and I was in complete shock mode.

First, my mom told her side of the story. According to her, I was uncontrollable, and had run away from home, and I was only 15. I hitchhiked all the time, was working at The Source Restaurant at night, skipping school, and occasionally stealing the family station wagon for joyrides. She wasn't wrong. These stories were mostly true.

Magus then told my story to the judge. He painted a different picture of me, coming from my childhood. He went on to talk about my mom, telling the court that she was a neglectful mother—there was lots of yelling in the family, and no supervision. Mom worked six days a week, and when we kids woke up in the morning, she was still passed out and gave us no help to get ready for school. She got home from work at 10 p.m. and was always drinking at night. On Sundays she slept in until 2 p.m. For all intents and purposes, all four of us sisters were on our own and left to fend for ourselves.

Magus said that I wanted to be in a warm and loving environment, such as The Source Family. And that I was thriving and happy, and did not want to go back to my home life. In addition, he let it be known that I had already taken the G.E.D. test, therefore I had no obligation to return to high school. My mom had no idea about this, and it seemed to totally undercut her argument.

I thought that Magus took it easy on my mom. There were many more stories of a bad homelife. So many memories flashed in my mind—which, had the judge known about them, would have been bad for my mom.

I had so much love and support from The Source, I'm not sure she would relate to this kind of love. Up until the time I spent in The Source Family, I thought I led a normal life, and everyone lived this way. Now I knew there was something better for me. The Source Family Commune.

Then my mom started talking, saying that she had no control over me, that I ran away from home, and I joined this commune without her permission. And the more my mom spoke and rambled on, the less the judge seemed to be convinced of her mental stability.

To me, it was all a blur, and I could barely hear anything that was being said. All I know is that something didn't feel right. Before I knew it, the judge had made a decision to declare that my mom was an unfit parent and that I would become a "ward of the court."

I asked Magus, "What does that mean?"

He replied, "I'm not sure what that means, so I'm going to find out."

Magus spoke with the judge and found out that what it meant was that the court would now make all decisions about where I would go and what I would do. My mother was no longer my legal guardian. My mom was shocked and freaking out. She was yelling at her attorney, "Why did you let this happen!?" her arms dramatically flailing.

This wasn't what was supposed to happen. I didn't know which option was worse: being a ward of the court, or having to return to be with my mom.

Moments later, a social worker came to greet me and gave me a synopsis of what was about to happen. She told me that I was going to be taken to Juvenile Hall while they figured out what to do with me. At this point, I was crying and confused, and in shock.

Magus told me, "Don't worry, I'll get you out of there."

I was escorted by a bailiff and the social worker into a van and taken to Juvenile Hall in Los Angeles.

We arrived at Juvenile Hall and I was in utter disbelief. Earlier that morning, I was in the Mother House in a beautiful environment meditating, and now I was here.

When I arrived, the first thing that they did was take a photo of me—then they fingerprinted me and then led me to the shower area. They told me to take my clothes off, and they searched me for God-knows-what—I had no idea.

The women officers, dressed in uniform, were tough, orderly, and intimidating. I did exactly as I was told, and took all my clothes off, and stood naked in the middle of a huge shower. They ran the water and I was completely embarrassed. I was so scared about the unknown. My heart was beating super fast and my breath was heavy. I thought I might pass out any minute. I tried my hardest not to. I needed to stay calm, use my breath and gain control to survive. This by far was the heaviest experience of my young life.

Next I was to put on my own uniform, which consisted of orange pants and an orange top. I had no personal belongings with me, so that was not an issue. I started to feel completely strange. I felt traumatized.

Then I was led to the sleeping quarters, where all the other girls were. I remember there being approximately 20 sets of bunk beds, full of young girls my age. They too were wearing all orange uniforms. I was left there with the girls and sat down on a bed, and soon was surrounded by a large group of girls, all asking me why I was there, and what badass thing did I do?

Some of the girls already had tattoos on their bodies. Most of them were scary and acting tough. A few girls didn't look like they belonged there, like me. They were very quiet and withdrawn. I wondered why these girls were there? What heinous crime did they commit? I couldn't tell them my story because it wasn't bad, or so I thought.

After talking to these girls, I knew that I had to survive this unfortunate situation, and thank God I was a little street smart from growing up in West Hollywood, and being on my own.

I started asking questions—why were they there? I wanted to get the attention off of me. Next thing I know, a bell rings. The girls pushed me in line, saying "You have to stand in line to go to the cafeteria for dinner."

I was completely and emotionally exhausted from the experience. While I was walking in line, I started feeling hot and dizzy. Everything suddenly went black and I fainted. I fell and hit my head on a door, getting a huge cut above my left eyebrow that started bleeding profusely everywhere—and I was totally unconscious. (I still have that scar today above my eyebrow that serves as a reminder of my time in juvie.)

Sometime afterwards, I woke up in the nurses ward, and the nurses told me what happened. I was the only one there—there were approximately 8 beds—and I was it. I had bandages on my head, and was in shock. How did I get here?

The next day, the social worker came to see me. She told me that I did not belong in juvenile hall—and that she would find a better situation for me. I couldn't even talk or express myself. I just prayed that I would be able to get out of there.

She asked me if I wanted any visitors, and I said that I would love to have anyone in The Source Family to come and visit me. She said that it would not be allowed. She asked if I would like my mother to come visit me, and I adamantly said no. It was her fault I was here.

There was a big window where I could see everyone who came through the guard gate to juvenile hall—and I noticed Jim (Father) trying to come and visit me, and they turned him away. I just cried and prayed. I think other Family members tried to visit me but they were all turned away. I wondered how many people knew what had just happened to me. I know that Magus, my mom and Father knew what happened.

The Halfway House

I stayed in the nurse ward for a week, recovering from my fall. The social worker came back and said, "I found a place for you. It's a Halfway House." I asked her what that meant, and why I was going there. I knew this was not going to be a journey that I was used to.

She explained to me that it was a home where I would get psychological counseling, and rehabilitation, until they figure out what else is going to happen. She told me that the next step from a Halfway House would be a foster home. Now I knew that I was off the path. I had to figure out how to survive, once again. I knew that I had to become a strong person. It would put my strengths to the test.

The social worker was there every day talking to me, saying that I didn't belong there. I didn't question her, or barely talk. I was silent and didn't even respond—in complete shock. Then she drove me in her car to the valley, in Sherman Oaks, to the Halfway House. The institution looked like a huge one-story, sterile office building. You walked in the front door to the reception, and the entry to the rooms was behind lock and key, like a jail. All of the windows looked out into a central courtyard. Girls lived on one side, boys on the other, separated by a locked door. There were lots of crazy people and drug addicts. I wasn't either—but I guess I fit in, because I wanted to join a commune.

My new roommate Annie had psychological issues. One of the first nights I was there, I was awakened by the sound of Annie screaming bloody murder, having a manic episode. The next thing I knew, several staff rushed in to subdue her in a straight jacket, then removed her and brought her to solitary confinement. Annie continued screaming her head off for what seemed like hours, keeping everyone awake, including me. In a weird way, I felt somewhat responsible for Annie being in this predicament— maybe it was because she was yelling my name. Later I found out that it was her psychological instability.

I realized that I had to survive, and quickly. I was not going to be getting out anytime soon. I wasn't allowed to see anybody, at first. I needed to blend in the best that I could. I was very quiet and I didn't participate in the group counseling sessions. But eventually I had to, or else it would have been even more difficult for me to survive. As I felt more comfortable, I started participating, and I learned about myself and other people. I learned that I wanted to be in The Source Family even more. It built within me an even stronger conviction.

I became friends with the Counselor guy (we'll call him "John"). John helped me sort out my emotions and a lot of things that I couldn't talk to anybody about. But I still had to stick with their program and follow their guidelines—which were to engage in the group counseling sessions, and no drugs, sex or leaving the institution.

Soon I was allowed visitors. But I still didn't want to see my mom—I was angry with her. Friends started visiting me, with special permission. They would come from high school, begging me not to join The Source Family and to come back to school.

John the Counselor had a lot of the power. He decided who could visit me, and when. He could tell how sad I was and how emotional it was to be away from everybody in The Family. He started letting them come visit me. Ramacharaka came to visit me, and after not seeing him for so much time, it was a case of 'absence makes the heart grow fonder.'

My sister Marcia (Mate / Blessing) never came. She was also underage, and concerned about herself. Later she told me that she would come with Pythias, her then-boyfriend, and watch me out in the yard when I visited with others. Different Source Family members came to visit, as much as was allowed.

My ex-boyfriend Bart, Jim's biological son, contacted my mother to find out where I was and what happened. My mom explained what happened and told him how to get in contact with me. Bart came to visit me, at one point, and we sat in the garden. He tried to talk me out of going back to The Source Family. Bart had been a part of The Family for a nanominute, but he didn't really understand what it was all about. Why was he trying to talk me out of it? Maybe because he cared about me a lot and was concerned that I was giving too much of my life away. He thought that I was being brainwashed to think a certain way, and not be my own self.

Because of Bart not wanting me to join The Family, I didn't talk to him very much—I was very quiet. In fact, if anyone tried to convince me to leave The Source Family, I would totally shut down.

Everyone thought it was really weird to join a commune. I didn't talk very much about it. I was in complete shock the entire time. When people visited me, they did the talking. I thought,

"This is my world now." I was following all the rules and guide-lines in the situation that I was in, and praying that something was going to happen to help me.

They had a library of books there, and I read most of them. One of the books that stood out was the story of *Siddhartha*—a quest for enlightenment by the founder of Buddhism. I had this book in my hand when Pythias came to visit me, and he secretly slipped a note inside the book. The note read: "Try to get to a Sunday morning meditation, and all will be OK.—Father."

I was so scared to get this note. Would I be found out, and get in (bigger) trouble? I didn't know what the plan was—all I knew is that I had to find a way to get to a Sunday morning meditation. It took me a while to convince the counselor to take me to a Sunday morning meditation. I don't know how I did this, but I was able to convince him to go with me and see what I had experienced. There was no way that I could have possibly conceived what Father had planned.

The Great Escape

Winter 1973

Stranded in the Halfway House, I had a lot of time to think. My questions were often aimed at God. "God please explain to me why I so badly want to be with this commune." I knew I felt so incredibly good when I was there, and I loved Ramacharaka, Father Yod and all my spiritual brothers and sisters, especially my biological sister Blessing (Marcia).

I also knew that I didn't want to be back at my mom's house, or should I say, I was no longer allowed to be there. I was concerned that the next step would be a foster home with "Piscean strangers" who wouldn't accept me. (In The Source Family, we were all evolved and living in the Age of Aqaurius—we were Aquarians. Thus, Pisceans were any non-spiritual outsiders who went about living unenlightened 'normal lives' outside of our Family—according to the teachings of Father.) I had to convince John the counselor to take me to The Mother House as soon as possible for a morning meditation. I had no idea what was in store for me. Was Father Yod up to something?

During one of our private counseling sessions, I finally felt comfortable bringing up going to a Sunday morning meditation. I was so nervous bringing anything up about The Source Family. It took a lot of courage for me to stand up for myself. Up until that moment, I'd just listened to my counselor and rarely gave my opinion. I tried so hard to understand why I wanted so badly to be in The Source Family. For a moment I thought that I was a bad person for wanting to be in the commune. I had questioned myself repeatedly—"Why?"

I'm happy to say that I was able to convince John to go with me to a Sunday morning meditation at The Mother House. He was intrigued and fascinated by my story, and I think he did some research on The Source and was curious himself.

I had never been so nervous to go see everyone, especially Ramacharaka and Father. I woke up early that Sunday, dressed in my white skirt and top. I wore a silver belt with turquoise and jade on it. I put on my birkenstocks and brushed my long golden brown hair. My nerves were flying with excitement and I could hear my heart beating so fast. I didn't care—I was about to be a part of class. I hadn't been there for many months (seemed like an eternity)—since the courtroom showdown with my mom, the nurse ward, and the Halfway House.

I was a little concerned how John would take all this in. I was praying that he wouldn't make us leave early because he thought it wasn't good for me. We talked in the car about how everything happened at the meditation class. I tried to prepare him and begged him to be open minded and give this a chance. It concerned me that pot (marijuana, aka The Sacred Herb) was going to be smoked and this was illegal. But this was a part of our ritual and it wasn't going to change just because we were coming.

We finally arrived at The Mother House at 4:00 a.m. We could hear the beautiful sound of angels singing from the car. My heart was jumping and I was so excited. As we pulled up Ramacharaka was waiting for us outside. I greeted him with a hug and squeeze. I was so happy to be there and couldn't wait to experience a morning meditation and see Father Yod.

Ramacharaka escorted us through the doors and into the meditation room. All my brothers and sisters were sitting in lotus positions chanting. Mostly their eyes were closed and they didn't see me come in. Ramacharaka led us to the front, right in front of where Father was going to sit and lead class. I had never sat this close to him before—I always sat in the middle back with Ramacharaka.

John was dressed in jeans and a plaid shirt. He stood out like a sore thumb. John couldn't sit in a lotus position and struggled to find a comfortable way to sit.

At about 4:30 a.m. Father and his three main women Makushla, Ahom and Prism walked into the room. Father's presence was like no other. He was tall and magnetic, emanating an aura of bright light. He wore a white shawl over his white shirt and white pants, and he was barefoot (as we all were—there were no shoes in the House / Temple). As Father walked in, we kept chanting.

As soon as I saw Father I wanted to leap into his arms and beg him to rescue me from this horrible nightmare. This was the first time I had seen him in several months. When Father sat down, I was in front of him and he reached out for me to come to him. I immediately jumped into his arms. I felt so loved by him and secure that all would be okay. I didn't want to leave.

At this time, all my brothers and sisters saw me. *Shewww* was all I heard. No one really knew what I'd been through, just a few people. Class started as usual and John participated to the best of his ability. He was a trooper. I felt like I was in heaven and exactly where I belonged. No more questions—just answers as to why I wanted this.

Father's sermon was all about me, in an esoteric sense. I knew exactly what he was talking about. I wished I was free to be there and didn't have this legal matter preventing me from being with my family here. For about an hour, I forgot about my predicament.

Once meditation class was over and everyone dispersed into their duties, Father asked John and I to stay for a while. I was so happy John agreed, and he, Ramacharaka and I were left alone with only Makushla and Father. At first Father just asked John questions about himself. Then it led to what his thoughts were about The Family and class. I got a little anxious because I knew it was getting close to the time I would have to leave.

Things started to change to a different tone. Father got confrontational with John. My mind was a blur and I was so stunned I can't remember exactly what Father said. He talked to John and explained the philosophy of The Source Family, saying that it would be in my best interests for me to be there. He told John that letting me go would be doing a good thing—and he would incur good karma. Father called John his son and convinced John to set me free.

Ramacharaka and I knew nothing about Father's plans. We were both so confused and not sure of what his plans were. We both only knew that Father was so unpredictable and we would go along with it.

The next thing I knew, John came over to me and gave me a hug, and wished me well, and then he walked out the door. It was a surprise to me that John agreed and left without me. What was happening? Now my nerves were completely going crazy.

One of the women brought out a suitcase for me, all packed with clothes, money and meditation tapes. There was a limousine waiting outside for me. I was to move fast because Father had a plan for me to escape. It was explained to me that I was going to hide out for a couple of months and wasn't to have any contact with any Family members. I was going to stay with a family that were friends of Jim. They didn't want to tell me where and who.

I was to stay away from society and just hide out for now. Future instructions would be delivered to me by my host family. I couldn't believe what I was hearing. I was scared to death that I was running away from the law. I trusted Father and went along with his plan without thinking of the consequences. I hugged Ramacharaka and Father goodbye. The driver opened the door for me and I hesitantly went inside. I couldn't imagine where he was taking me. I just trusted Father and had faith that it would work out.

The drive to who-knew-where was scary. The driver wore a black hat that looked like a policeman. He was quiet and authoritative. He was also a Piscean (non-Family, an outsider) and a stranger. I was uncomfortable and worried. I kept looking out the window thinking that at any moment a police car was going to stop the limo and put me in jail for breaking the law. I didn't even talk to the driver and ask him where we were going. The drive seemed long and surreal. It seemed like hours, but it was only two hours until we arrived at our destination. All I knew is that it was in the mountains not too far from Los Angeles.

The family came out to greet me and escorted me into the house quickly. To this day I can't remember my host family names. It was a husband and wife and I think they had a child. They were friends of Jim and did him a big favor by hiding me. I felt like I was in a movie and this wasn't really happening. I went to my bedroom completely blown away that this was for real. I walked inside to find two twin beds and a nightstand in between the beds. It was on the bottom floor, like a basement below the main house. I opened my suitcase to find all these tapes of morning meditation classes and beautiful "Piscean clothes." No white clothes! There was also cash and letters from some family members. Now I knew this was real and I had to survive once again.

I realized that I had never before slept in a bedroom by myself. I felt so lonely. As time went on, I stayed mostly in my bedroom. I had very little contact with the host family. They were strangers to me and I was quite shy. They were nice and took very good care of me, but I didn't really get to know them, and I had no choice but to trust them.

I would wake up early in the morning, put on a meditation tape and have my own meditation class. It kept me sane. I wrote many letters to Father and Ramacharaka. I knew the letters wouldn't get mailed, but I wanted to write to them anyway. I walked everyday in the woods with tall pine trees—always alone in the woods—along with the birds, dragonflies, and squirrels. I loved the smell of the pine trees.

Eventually I meandered into town and saw a sign that told me I was in Idyllwild—a small mountain community of a couple thousand people just outside of Los Angeles, with few businesses and houses. I remembered camping near there when I was 12 years old, with Bart, his best friend Craig, Tamara (Craig's sister and my close friend at the time), and Mary, Craig's mother.

Time seemed to move so slowly and I couldn't wait to see what the plan was next. I was always afraid that someone was going to come get me and put me in jail. The whole time I was there, I barely said a word. I kept to myself and tried to be a good guest—my room was perfectly clean all the time. I was so traumatized by the whole experience of going to court, being put in juvenile hall, living in a Halfway House, and having therapy daily, all because of my spiritual beliefs.

It had been over two months since I arrived in Idyllwild— but it seemed like an eternity. I wasn't exactly sure how long it had been. At last the day came when the host family instructed me that I was getting picked up the next morning and taken somewhere else. They didn't know where—only that I had to be packed and ready by 9:00 a.m.

The next morning I was told to dress in this tie-dye velvet dress and put on a wig. I looked so Piscean and was so uncomfortable in the disguise. I was to look like someone else—just in case someone was looking for me—but I was very concerned that I would be noticed. The same limousine and same driver from before picked me up. I felt somewhat comfortable because I recognized him—but still very insecure about what might happen next. After all, I was still a fugitive.

I said my goodbyes to the family and thanked them for hiding me. I once again jumped into the limo and we drove off. The first time I had been in the limo, I hadn't said a single word. I was traumatized and in shock. This time around, I was able to find my voice and I asked the driver, "Where are we going?"

He answered that he was taking me to LAX Airport and that I was going on an airplane to Hawaii. I was thinking: I've never been on a plane and I've never been outside of California. He gave me an ID, lots of cash, and a letter from Father. He walked me to the gate and made sure I got on the airplane safely. I got situated in my seat and gazed out the window as we took off over the Pacific en route to the islands and the great unknown.

Sitting in my seat, located one aisle from the smoking section of the plane—I was supposedly in the 'non-smoking' section. Over the course of five hours on the flight I kept flashing back to my mom chain-smoking—reminding me how much I hated cigarettes. At the Halfway House, I had asked God to get me out.

God had listened. Now here I was, at age 15, after all that I had been through, a fugitive headed to Hawaii.

I opened the letter from Father. It read: "Dear Nirvana, you are going to the island of Maui. Venus will pick you up. She will watch over you until the rest of the people come. Venus's job is to look for land for us to live. It may be a few months, then we will come. Stay incognito."

Father Yod demonstrating archery at The Father House
(L to R: Tahuti, Snow, Ramacharaka, Pythias,
my sister Blessing)

Chapter 4

GONE TO MAUI

Island Time

Spring 1973

My flight arrived at Maui's Kahului Airport around 10:30 p.m. It was dark out, practically the middle of the night. As I walked off the plane, the first thing that struck me was the smell of flowers. A beautiful perfume fragrance overtook me.

I couldn't believe I was in Hawaii all by myself. I had just left Idyllwild, in a limousine for the second time. The driver had put me on this plane in a disguise to a faraway island. Craziness.

My mind was numb with random thoughts. So far my teenage life has been a whirlwind. I left my earth family and my spiritual family behind. I soon had to get back to reality and get into survival mode again. The get up that I was wearing was really bothering me. I felt so uncomfortable and Piscean.

Since this was my first time on a plane or at an airport, I didn't know what to do. I followed the other passengers to an area called Baggage Claim. Everything was outdoors. This was apparently not the typical airport. I got my one suitcase and carried it to where everyone else was going out front. I saw people getting picked up by cars, taxis, and buses. I wasn't sure how Venus would recognize me in this disguise.

I waited and waited and found a bench which was outside by the area where cars would pull up. The luggage conveyor belt was just behind. As I sat there alone, I started thinking about what just happened. Escaping Los Angeles in a disguise wearing 'normal people' clothes, and a wig, and with more money than I've ever seen.

Suddenly it all hit me. I felt a little scared. Most of all I felt lonely. I yearned for The Family and wondered if and when I'd ever see them again. It had been months. I was still as devoted as ever. If Father said this is what I had to do, I knew everything would be ok.

I snapped out of it when the low murmur of the luggage belt stopped—now it was silent. Then the lights behind went off. Just the glow of the street light was left. I had to get out of there and fast.

I looked around for Venus, who was nowhere to be found. I waited out front, thinking that she would arrive at any moment. And I waited. And waited. And soon the airport was virtually empty, except for me and the janitor. I asked the janitor if there was a payphone anywhere. He showed me a payphone, and I called Venus. In Father's letter he had included her number and address.

Venus answered the phone, half-asleep and all groggy. "Uh . . . hello?"

I asked, "Where are you? I've been waiting for hours at the airport."

She said, "Take a taxi. Here's the address. I'll leave the front door open. Go inside, and take a right—that's your bedroom."

I was like, "Really?" Here I was in a totally new place and didn't know anyone there. I felt so alone and confused and scared—a stranger in a strange land, thousands of miles from home.

I went back to the janitor and he called me a taxi. Moments later I watched as the taxi came rolling towards me through the empty airport. I looked at the driver, and realized that I was about to get into a car with a complete stranger, while I was holding a suitcase full of cash. Did I have any other option? I averted my eyes from his glare and tried my best to act normal and keep my composure. Survival mode. I stepped into the car and gave the driver the address in Lahaina, about forty-five minutes away from the airport.

Off we went. On the ride there I breathed in the warm smell of the ocean as we curved around mountains, catching glimpses of the moon shining on the water. At last the driver dropped me off and I got out and walked to the front door, where I was met by Venus, who was somewhat awake. She pointed to the room.

I wanted to scream and yell in frustration, but by this point I was so exhausted and just headed to bed. In the bedroom, there was nothing. Just a futon. I put my suitcase down, threw off the wig and the Piscean clothes, lay down and passed out asleep on the futon.

The next morning, I leisurely woke up, feeling very guilty that I had missed morning meditation. My first experience with jetlag. I jumped up and opened the door. Peeking out, I heard Venus in the kitchen.

I approached Venus and confronted her: "What happened?"

She said, "Don't have such an ego about it. Don't be on an ego trip."

At this point, Venus was older than me and I looked up to her. I decided to just get over it and move on. I was pondering if I should tell Father about this little mishap or not, but I chose not to.

I quickly realized that I was free and on my own, and that there was no one here to supervise or guide me. I felt like a free person for the first time in my life. In order to survive, again, I chose to continue with Father's philosophy every morning, do my exercises, stay vegetarian, and live life while waiting for whatever might come next.

Lonely in Lahaina

Now I was on my own wandering around Lahaina, a small village outside of Kaanapali, a tourist resort. The neighborhood was mostly locals, surfers, fisherman, Japanese, and mainland folk. The houses were moderate, modest, humble homes. Papaya, avocado, and mango trees were everywhere. You could just walk down the street and pick ripe fruit off the ground. Sometimes there were boxes of fruit sitting at the end of the driveways saying "free for the taking." The weather was hot most of the time and humid.

If I just walked a few blocks towards the ocean, the businesses for the tourists were plenty. The harbor had some fishing boats, yachts, and tourist whale watching boats. I loved walking to the harbor and watching the boats sail off to the horizon. People were walking in droves on the small streets of Lahaina. It was full of hippies living out of their vans and tents on the beaches. In the beginning of town was a huge banyan tree in a park. It was said to be the largest of its kind in all of Hawaii. I often would take a journal and write my thoughts and quotes while under this massive tree.

I was always trying to fill the day up with adventure. I was lonely in Lahaina. I didn't know if I should socialize with anyone or stay quiet and to myself. I still wasn't comfortable being on my own. I always had to look behind my back and see if anyone recognized me from Los Angeles. After all, I was a fugitive.

I started to meet a few hippies at the Music and Art Festivals. There's one in particular that I had a little fling with. He had dark brown hair longer than mine—even though he wasn't in The Family, he looked like he could be "one of us." He lived in his van and traveled the island. He was educated and smart—I think he was a Stanford guy (although at the time I didn't even know what Stanford was). He just wanted a break from the mainland and to be free. We had this in common.

We became friends and he listened to my story. I really needed someone to talk to. He became that person. We had a one night stand, as the Piscean world calls it. After that the friendship was over. He was not in The Family and I couldn't pursue it. Totally against the rules.

For the first couple months on Maui, I was with only Venus (other than the fling)—just the two of us living in the same house. Every so often I would run into Venus out in town, but she wasn't very social with me. I wasn't sure what was going on with her and The Family, but she didn't seem to be into it, like I was.

After I was in Maui for a few months, Father sent America, Minerva and her two children to come to Maui and look for land to rent or buy for the Family to live. This was supposed to be Venus's job, but that didn't happen. America and Minerva also came to get me and take care of me. As soon as they arrived in Maui, we all stayed in a small hotel in Lahaina. Immediately we started to scope out land and a house for us to live in. We drove all around Maui daily until we found a property. Up until then, I had not been anywhere on the island but Lahaina.

Maui is a beautiful Island. Waterfalls, mountains, beaches, and the massive Haleakala volcanic crater. I had never seen such green and lush mountains. We eventually found a ranch-style house on a huge piece of property in Haiku above Makawao—a tiny hippie town, later famous for its Hawaiian cowboys (pani-olos). We told Father and The Family about it and sent photos. He loved it and gave us his blessing to move forward. We signed the lease, left the hotel, and moved into the house. A long dirt driveway led to the house, which also had a hut and plenty of room to start a garden.

By this time, I was feeling really homesick. I missed Ramach-araka. We had only been together for a short time before I was taken away. In Maui, I had lots of free time to think and dream about what our relationship could be like in the future when we reunited.

The first person who flew to Maui to be with me was Ram-acharaka, who Father had now given the new name of Starman. I was so happy to see him. He came to Maui with Ocean, Water-fall, Sancia, Palm, Ra, and many other members, who Father sent over to start a farm and grow vegetables. We mostly ate only indigenous foods. One of the indigenous foods was breadfruit. It tasted like a potato (but slightly more revolting) and grew all over the island.

When Starman came, we first stayed in the house with America and Minerva. Minerva had two kids and was pregnant with her third child. The house soon became overcrowded. We wanted our own space and privacy.

Starman built us a treehouse to live in—constructing it with a couple other brothers who had come over to prepare the land. Below the treehouse Starman made a makeshift kitchen. The treehouse had a ladder to climb up into, and there was just enough room for our bed and a little meditation area. Our treehouse in paradise. The good thing about the treehouse was that it was private.

Our Maui Treehouse

Mushroom Mountain

Father came to visit us on several occasions, with Makushla only, who was one of his three main women, and was Father's "Mother." Her pet name for him was "Kitty." Not many of us were in Maui yet, so when Father and Makushla came to visit, we got some quality alone time with him and it was amazing.

We had intimate meditations and conversations about how to live the best life—nutrition, meditation, relationships, and fulfilling our purpose. He told us that we should never cut the hair on any part of our body—it was our Cosmic Roots.

We often would hike down to the waterfall on the property. Wild mushrooms grew in the cow patties (aka dung). One day at the waterfall we all ate mushrooms. Apparently I had quite a trip that day. I wasn't used to drugs, and I had gotten really stoned. We all had. Trees were talking to me, rocks were dancing, and the waterfall was a kaleidoscope of different colors.

This is when Father changed my name from Nirvana to Mushroom. I now became a vegetable, due to this experience. It was dangerous to be the only vegetable in The Family, surrounded by vegetarians. And I never ate magic mushrooms again.

It was a fun time in Maui. I was 16 and I felt free and relaxed there—and safely far away from problems back home. In Hawaii, The Family wore relaxed clothing like a wrap with a bathing suit. The men wore sorongs and typically no shirts. It was a lot hotter and humid in Hawaii than Los Angeles. Long dresses and robes would not work here. I walked everywhere and went swimming in the ocean almost daily at beautiful Baldwin Beach—a spot popular with the locals for having picnics and barbeques.

We also took trips to Hana and hiked the Seven Sacred Pools. I remember being barefoot walking on the slippery rocky paths— it rained so much. In the pouring rain, we would still go up there and meditate when we got to the top. It was a whole day, hiking up to the top. Green ferns on the mountainside. Slush and mud everywhere. You had to be very careful while walking. Not many people went to the top—because it was so slippery. The goal was always to get to the top and meditate. We would swim naked in the pools along with a few other hippies.

It took three hours of driving slowly through the harrowing and treacherous roads. It rained a lot in Hana and waterfalls were everywhere. While driving we would often stop on the road where I could pick guavas, bananas, papayas, or starfruit right off the foliage, while we were still in the car.

Another trip was to Haleakala Crater, the volcano that formed Maui. We would drive up to the crater before the sunrise and watch the sun come up over the ocean. This was my favorite trip. The drive was an hour up a long winding road to the top. We left the house at 4:00 am to get to the observatory at the top of Haleakala Crater before the sunrise. It was always so cold so we had to be prepared.

There were always a few brave souls wanting to experience the sunrise. The sun came up over the Iao Valley with rays spraying over the mountains. Sometimes the clouds create a beautiful sunrise. We would all chant Omne, Omne as the sun appeared and soak in the warmth. Once the sun came up we would all go back down the mountain and start our day.

Morning meditation in Maui
From L to R: Minerva, Serenity, Waterfall, Palm,
Starman, and Mushroom (me)

A Stardust Is Born

Father told all the women to go to the Wailuku Civic Center to apply for food stamps. In order to get the food stamps, I used a fake ID, since I was still a fugitive, and I got a social security card with the name Mushroom Aquarian. I had to get a blood test, urine test, and a physical, and that's when they discovered that I was pregnant with Starman's baby.

I was only sixteen and not sure if I was ready for motherhood. It seemed that all my Family sisters were becoming pregnant too. Minerva reassured me that it was going to be okay. So I embraced being pregnant with all of my heart.

I have to admit I was scared to have a baby at sixteen. I trusted in Father and The Family that it would be okay. I was constantly asking different women what it was like to give birth. I was at Minerva's labor and learned as much as I could. Of course, she was a trained midwife, and her labor was mellow and beautiful. I could only pray that mine would be as well. I had heard that some of the births at The Mother House were very difficult. My sister Blessing's birth took three days.

Starman was making sure I only ate the purest foods and got exercise to have the most healthy baby. I was not allowed to have any dairy—we were vegan still. But all I did was crave ice cream. Starman thought that wasn't good for me—he was also a very disciplined nutritional eater. So ice cream was not an option. My diet consisted of fruits, vegetables, fish, and flatbread. I barely gained any weight and I didn't look pregnant until the last three months. My body was tiny and thin and the baby bump began to emerge like a basketball.

When I was about eight months into my pregnancy, I developed a severe iron deficiency. Because I never went to the doctors and I never had a check-up, I had no information on what I was experiencing and if it was OK or not. Father instructed me to eat chopped liver twice a day until I gave birth. At first I gagged, then I gradually started to like it. I ate iron rich foods, like dates and beets. Father had all the pregnant moms start drinking goat's milk and eating goat cheese and eggs. Temporarily non-vegan.

It was decided that I move into the main house for the end of my pregnancy. I was grateful to sleep in a more comfortable bed—being surrounded by Minerva, who was going to be my midwife, made me feel more secure about the upcoming delivery. But honestly, I was freaked out. I was only 16 at the time, and was very nervous and concerned. I knew there would be no doctor there and I would be doing this naturally. I wanted to get it over with.

In the evening of May 25, I started labor. I was about two weeks overdue, if they were correct in estimating the time. The first contraction came in the evening—I felt it in my abdomen, like a wave. Then it subsided. About 15 minutes later, another wave. My baby was on the way. It started off with very mild contractions, and my water never broke. It was a very nice and mellow transition, at first, and few people came into the room. Father, who had come to Maui from LA to visit us, was there and constantly checking in on me.

All my sisters set me up in the most beautiful space on a very comfortable bed on the floor, completely sterile. Hom (Aladdin) was playing the guitar and singing softly. Candles were lit and incense was burning. People were massaging my feet. It was very peaceful, and seemed like a long labor to me, about sixteen hours. In the last two hours, it seemed like there were dozens of Family members sitting around staring at my every move. I really just wanted all of them to leave. I only wanted Starman and Father to be there.

This was common practice for births in The Family—for everyone to partake in the births. Typically one of the midwives would deliver the baby. But in my case, Father would deliver my baby. This was beyond special. He was there for me. At the time, I didn't think that I was brave, but I must have been. If Father wasn't there, I don't know how I would have felt.

The Family birth rope—which had the names of all the babies born (so far) into The Family written onto cloth, numbered in order of birth dates—was brought into the room, put up, and attached to a hook on the ceiling. At first, I thought the birthrope was a silly and ridiculous idea. I was like, "I am not holding on that rope and squatting and having this baby." At the time I was thinking that I'm going to lay down and have the baby.

As the delivery drew closer, I realized that the birthrope would be my lifeline. I grabbed tightly onto a knot in the rope, and had two Family members supporting me, holding me up on each side. One of the two was always Starman. Awash with exhaustion, I could barely move or sit up on my own, and I was beginning to lose my grip on the rope.

Father had me, with the help of Starman and a few other brothers—hold on to the birth rope and squat. At that point, that is when I started making progress. The contractions became so intense that I could feel the pressure of this baby coming through. (All this with no drugs or medication.) All I wanted to do was push and get this baby out. It was either that, or I was going to die.

As the big moment drew closer, I got scared and thought to myself, "I should go to the hospital." However, Father made me feel secure that he would be with me and deliver my baby. I didn't think anything of it, because that's what we did. Father used to say that the Indians (Native Americans) gave birth at the top of a mountain under a tree, then they would come down the mountain with a baby. Seems simple enough.

I didn't know that I was having a girl and I was so happy when I was told it was a girl. My water broke as I was delivering her. She was born on May 26, 1974 at 2:38 p.m. with the amniotic sac over her whole body. Father said she was a saint born—and that in ancient times, saints were born with the sac on them.

She was born very healthy. Her birth was beautiful and serene (in retrospect). She had a little star on her head from the birthing, and Father named her Stardust. Her birth certificate would read: Stardust Aquarian—adopting the surname used by everyone else in The Family.

In line with keeping the birth natural, I had to bite the umbilical cord (to cut it) with my teeth. We did not use scissors or special tools to cut. Then Father took the cord and pushed all the nutrients down to Stardust's belly button and tied a knot. He must have stretched the cord a little too much, because Stardust had an outie belly button. Father said to take a sterile quarter and tape it directly onto her belly button for thirty days, and it would go back in. And sure enough, it did. The placenta was buried in the hillside—this was our practice for home births.

I was crying and laughing and shaking all at the same time from the blissfulness of it—it was the happiest, most amazing experience of my life. I was never so grateful that all went so well. Immediately after Stardust was born, she started to nurse. She took more nutrients from me. Fortunately, we would soon all be back to having dairy products again. After having her, my stomach was flat—I looked like a 12 year old. This was a few weeks before my 17th birthday.

I lucked out. Stardust was born at the right day, right time. Stardust got a beautiful fairy name. She was brought into this world in the most spiritual and loving way. She was the best baby and slept through the night right away. She never got sick. She loved to sleep. Laughing and happy. Everybody wanted to hold her and watch her. People would come up to her and engage. She was loving and easy going to everybody. Father Yahowah (as he came to be known) just loved her—constantly holding her and being with her. Everybody adored Stardust.

Once Stardust was born, my total focus was on her. Starman, in his role as a dad, was very hands on. He was totally committed to our relationship and being her father. They looked identical and I know he loved her very much. He was in heaven. I think he was also scared, like me—in a commune where you are not allowed to be attached to anything, or anyone, or have any ego.

At around this time May-September 1974, there were many babies born. My close sister Azure had Angel in May, Omega (aka

Anastasia) was expecting a baby in September, and I had Stardust May 26th.

The three new moms—Me, Anastasia (Omega), and Azure—would help each other by taking turns to watch the babies, like when others went to morning meditation. I would nurse any baby that I watched. I consciously made a decision to be the best mother I could possibly be—loving, attentive, and kind from day one.

Once I had a baby in the commune, things changed. We were called "the nursing mothers." It was our main focus to raise our babies and nurse on demand and be there for them one hundred percent of the time. We were excluded from many events. We leaned on each other for support and got very close. Anastasia and Azure were my closest sisters and we helped each other get through these difficult times. Sometimes we would nurse each others' babies.

It wasn't easy being a nursing mother and being so young. I didn't think anyone took me seriously and they left me out of the loop many times. Half the time I didn't know what was going on with the running of The Family or any legal logistics. I just blended in and did the best I could with following Father's teachings.

To produce and create more milk, we ate foods like alfalfa sprouts, sesame seeds, seaweed, and almonds. We would nurse anywhere—out in public—we wouldn't even cover up. Babies would reach into the blouse and grab a boob. We also fed babies—we gave them mashed avocados, bananas, rice cream, papaya—and introduced them to food as well. All the kids were vegetarians—we never ate meat.

I loved when Father would visit me and Stardust. He always said really nice things about Stardust. He always would hold her and hug her. Father would tell Stardust she was born a saint and was going to do good for humanity. She would always giggle at him and was happy all the time. She was so easy to be around people. Father loved that about her. Father gave so much love to us all. I always felt special with him.

A Stardust is Born with parents Mushroom (me, age 16) and Starman

Chapter 5

THE FATHER HOUSE

Return to the Mainland

Summer 1974

While I was in Maui I heard that The Family in Los Angeles had moved into a new house called "The Father House". The address was 2000 Nichols Canyon, overlooking the city of Los Angeles. This house was big, but not quite big enough for over one hundred plus Family members.

Father wanted all of the Family members who were in Maui, about 20 of us, to return to Los Angeles as soon as possible so that we could all be together again on the mainland. So once again we're off on an airplane back to Los Angeles—it would be a transition going from humid hot Hawaii to cooler climate LA.

When you walked in the front door of the Father House, it opened into a huge living room, where we had our morning meditations. Off to the left was a sizable kitchen and just outside the kitchen were several walk-in refrigerators. Outside was a pool and exercise equipment like the hanging bars. There was a garage that we converted into a music studio, where the band practiced their music and made records. We swam at 4:00 a.m. every day. The pool was freezing, but this didn't stop us.

When you went upstairs and walked down the hallway, all the bedrooms (except for Father's) were converted by the men, who engineered the rooms to make cubbies out of wood, divided into four sections—two on the bottom, two on the top. The cubbies measured 6 feet long, 3 feet wide, and 3 feet high. Inside the cubbies, there was just enough room to crawl in and sit up on the small bed. We made it work in the most creative way to fit in as many people as possible.

Once we arrived at the house, I was given a cubby to sleep in (with baby Stardust). In my section of cubbies, there were three other women with their babies—including Ahom, Father Yahowah's wife. Meanwhile Yahowah was in the master bedroom with Makushla. Yahowah's other eleven Council women were sleeping in cubbies as well throughout the house.

I have to say I didn't enjoy sleeping in a small confined space—where all you could do was sit up—it felt claustrophobic to me. I saw this living situation as another test of my strength. Yahowah would often tell us, "Life is a game. Everyone plays a part. How well you play the game is how you live your life." So I sucked it up and went with the program. Thankfully the cubby only lasted for one month.

Post-cubby I moved with Starman and Stardust into the Father House's ballroom, which we shared with several other couples—all with nursing mothers and newborn babies. (In April and May alone, eight babies had been born into The Family.) We all slept on padded roll-up mats on the floor, in sections about six feet wide.

In the ballroom there was enough space so that you could stand up and could walk (unlike life in cubby-land), so we were able to spread out more and have more room—which is probably the reason why we were all put together in there. It was relatively quiet in the ballroom, so the babies could nap at all hours of the day and night, even when there was "action" going on upstairs, which, of course, there often was.

One might expect that the ballroom would be constantly filled with the sounds of wailing babies—but the babies nursed so much (whenever they wanted—because Yahowah said that babies should be nursed "on demand"), they were happy campers and relatively calm. In the event of a baby having a crying fest, we would take them outside and walk them around, so as not to disturb the other Family members. All the mothers were dedicated 24/7 to motherhood.

Yahowah would often visit us in the ballroom, sitting in his chair by the fireplace, and we would hang out and talk. He shared his philosophy of how to raise a child—giving sermons on how to take care of your baby. Everyone would crowd around him and listen—not just the mothers and babies—other Family members would join as well. Yahowah loved holding Stardust and he vibed to her. She was adorable and always smiling, with a bubbly laugh. She was born with a positive radiance about her. I was so lucky that she was a good baby. Everyone wanted to hold her and play with her. For a while, I thought that all babies must be like that.

After about a month in the ballroom, we had yet another change-up. Three of the nursing mothers (Azure, Anastacia, and me) and our newborns Angel, Libra, and Stardust (but not their dads) would be moving out of the house and into the backyard.

Part of the reason for this was to make room for the new babies about to be born.

Our new abode would be a canvas dome tent, located up a pathway above the pool area at the foot of a mountain. The tent had enough room for three adults and three babies—and each of us brought a box with our personal belongings. Here we would have more privacy and space from the intensity of the house.

At night it was gently lit by the ambient landscape lighting. So if we needed to use the bathroom in the middle of the night, we had to walk into the house. In the tent we had more privacy—so there was less pressure if Stardust (or the other babies) made a sound or a noise. We could talk late into the night—and didn't feel like we were disturbing anybody. We took turns watching the babies—so that each of us could take turns going to morning meditation.

Even as I settled into motherhood and life in the Father House—in the back of my mind I was very nervous to be back in Los Angeles. I knew that I was a fugitive and it was a risk for me to stay in LA for very long. I knew that I never wanted to go back to that Halfway House. I was also concerned that I would be put in Juvenile Hall because I escaped.

I had no idea what the legal system would do to me if they found me—and this time around, it wasn't just me I was concerned about—what would happen to Stardust? I also prayed that no one in my family or high school would see or recognize me. I had to lay low and keep an alert out at all times. Meanwhile, no one in The Source Family knew what had happened to me—because we lived in the Now, and that was the Past.

Every morning without fail we had our meditation classes

at 4:30 a.m. Father would walk down the stairs with Makushla on one side and Ahom on the other side and Prism behind him. Father always had a smile on his face and seemed to acknowledge everyone personally in the room as he passed by. It was one of his many talents. He had a bright light surrounding him and walked with so much confidence and love in his eyes. I was so in love with Father Yod in a daughterly way. He was my main reason for being in The Family and devoting myself to his philosophy of how to live the most natural life.

Stitching Together

While the single women were out working at The Source Restaurant, the nursing mothers with children stayed home and sewed and took care of the babies. Father taught us that the child should be with his mother until he was seven years old—the first septenary of their life. (It was Father's belief that every septenary, the brain reached a milestone.) This philosophy allowed us mothers to be totally devoted to our babies.

By the time we all moved back to Los Angeles, we changed our wardrobe. We now wore dresses with all different fabrics and colors. We often used white homespun velvets, and cotton materials. Our dresses were always sexy and form-fitting. I always felt like a goddess wearing long dresses. The men added color to their robes too. They still wore long robes with sashes around their waist.

Our days were filled with sewing and making clothes for the men and women. Basically all of our clothes were sewn by us. We all got very creative and I'm grateful to have learned such a craft.

This was a special time for the women and I cherished it very much. We were always hugging, kissing, and complimenting each other—it was this beautiful, positive energy that attracted me to The Family.

The House of Fabrics in West Hollywood was our constant excursion. We bought all the homespun material we could find. We had a huge sewing club. This became a big challenge for me, because I was one of the women who knew nothing about sewing. Azure—who was one of my best friends in The Family—was a professional tailor, and she was also five years older than me. She taught us all what to do.

My job was to make clothes for me, Starman, and Stardust. I also sewed blankets for Stardust with silk satin and velvet fabrics. We also bought beautiful ribbons to sew on the dresses. Father's women made clothes for him and also for themselves. Another craft we all took part in was beading. There was this great beading store on Fairfax called Jo-El's. We made necklaces and headbands and also embroidered and beaded the dresses for a little flare.

Yahowah's Stories

After our intense meditations—full of breathing exercises, chanting, smoking the sacred herb, and visualization—I looked forward to Father's captivating stories about his life before The Family.

He talked often about his sons—Beau, Bart and Ben—and his wife of fifteen years, their mother Elaine. He would say how much he loved her and regrets hurting her and letting her down. When Jim and Elaine first started dating, and before they got married, he told her that he had something to disclose: "Elaine, I am really concerned about something. I have never been faithful to any woman in my life." Monogamy was not his strong suit. He was a womanizer and a wanderer. But Elaine didn't believe that Jim would ever be unfaithful to her—she had nothing but love in her mind, going forward. And at first, he was devoted to her.

Two stories that stood out were about the two times in his early life when he had killed men in self-defense, using his judo and jujutsu skills, to defend himself and to protect his wife, Elaine. Yahowah seemed to be emphasizing to us the importance of being able to defend yourself—and that the men had to protect the women. Yahowah was also sending a message: "Don't mess with me."

Yahowah told us, "Elaine and I were living in a small cabin, with our newborn son Beau, in Topanga Canyon. Our neighbor was going out of town and wanted us to watch his dog for a couple of weeks while he was away. I gladly obliged. When the neighbor returned, he found out that we had let the dog sleep outside of our cabin during the evenings. This was not to our neighbor's liking. In fact, he became enraged—one thing led to another, and he proceeded to violently attack me. I had to defend myself and Elaine – and I went on autopilot and responded automatically. With a swift judo chop to the neck, I sent him to the ground, with a broken trachea, and he passed away on the spot. When the police came, I was brought to jail, where I stayed overnight. Since I was acting in self-defense, I was released the next morning and not charged."

The second time, a jealous husband of Jean Ingram, a popular TV star—a woman that Jim was "seeing" (aka an affair)—showed up in Jim's office above The Aware Inn restaurant in the middle of the morning, with a gun. He was in a jealous rage and threatened to kill him. Jim thought fast and defended himself, delivering numerous judo chops to the neck of the intruder. Then the intruder's gun went off, and Jim killed the man in self-defense. The story became the talk of Hollywood and was publicized daily because the woman was a celebrity and it was a media frenzy. Jim was arrested, because it was his second murder offense.

Elaine stood by her man, hired the best lawyer she could find, and worked tirelessly 24 hours a day to prove him innocent. Elaine showed up to every court appearance and helped in eventually getting him free of the murder charges. Jim would be sentenced to jail and serve time for one and a half years.

During his time in jail, Jim realized that he needed to change himself. It was then that he read The Bible and learned Eastern philosophy. Elaine would visit him and bring Bart and Ben, and the boys would play outside in a location where Jim could see them from his jail cell window.

A consequence of his murder trial was he was not allowed to own the Aware Inn and have a liqour license. It was at this time Jim opened up the Old World Restaurant and gave the Aware Inn and their beautiful house at the top of Laurel Canyon solely to Elaine.

Elaine gave him one more chance to be faithful to her, but Jim couldn't be faithful (she caught him upstairs above the Old World Restaurant with another woman) and Elaine divorced him. Shortly after many failed affairs, Jim started going to Yogi Bhajan classes (a master of the Sikh religion) and soon became Yogi Bhajan's most devoted disciple.

Father's stories were legendary about his time in the war. We heard story after story about World War 2. One story stood out from his wartime experiences—when Jim was just about to receive a Congressional Medal of Honor for his service in the Marines. The night before receiving the medal, he had a confrontation with his Commander. The Commander was pushing Jim's buttons about his mother (even though he had no idea about Jim's sensitivity).

Why was Jim so sensitive about his mother, Cora? Growing up during the Great Depression, Jim's father left when Jim was about 3 or 4 years old, so it was Jim and his mom against the world. His mother became a maid to make ends meet. At age five, Jim was a 'newsie"—selling newspapers on the corners—and oftentimes other kids would beat the crap out of him to take his place on the best street corners. It was a rough upbringing. Sufficiently triggered, Jim got into a major fight with the Commander. In retaliation, the Commander put Jim in a holding cell (the brig) on the ship. And consequently Jim did not receive the medal.

The stories were many and seemed endless. After morning meditations, reality took place. We all had chores and jobs to do. Sometimes Father would go upstairs to his room and continue telling stories to a small group of us. I enjoyed listening to Father talk about his past.

The Leader of the Band

Music was becoming more important to Father. He would say that music is the universal language, channeling feel-good energy and vibrations. The Family band was rehearsing, recording, and playing gigs at local high schools and colleges. I think Father was using music to spread his message (come join The Family and be a part of the Aquarian Age) and also trying to recruit young Family members.

What kind of music was it? In the beginning of The Family, a few years earlier, the music was more of a Joni Mitchell style, with acoustic roots. But by this point, it had evolved into a heavy psychedelic, improvisational, noise rock . . . with Father "singing" and rapping over the top—and occasionally banging a gong. The music was like a jam session—loud, and not necessarily on beat. Sunflower and Arlick were in professional bands before The Family. Arlick was in The Seeds and Sunflower was in another professional band that was on the verge of getting signed.

In our Family there were a ton of talented musicians, artists, and crafts-makers, many at the pro level who knew what they were doing. We had an in-house production team, par excellence—they knew the mechanics and engineering of the music and performance worlds, so they set everything up in an amazing way.

I sometimes wondered to myself—what is my talent? I was observing the talent—trying to learn what my place was in the world. I admired so many people in The Family. I gravitated to the positivity.

However, it seemed to me that we started spending more money on the band than on the rest of The Family's essential needs. But it made Father so happy for him to be in the band. He loved doing it. Whatever he wanted to do—we all helped him achieve it.

Father wanted a Rolls Royce to drive around in, so one of the women went out and was able to lease a brand new Rolls Royce. This car brought so much joy to Father—and I thought it was pretty cool. Pythias became his chauffeur and drove all of us around Hollywood and LA, including me and Stardust. Whenever we would go to an outing or event for the music, there would be a Rolls Royce leading the way, with twelve VW vans following behind, like a presidential procession. It was quite a sight to see. Everyone would stare at us and wonder who the heck we were.

One day, Father wanted all the women in The Family to pose for the cover of the band's new record album. He wanted us all to stand around the Rolls Royce. I think Father wanted to show off his success by taking a photo of all the beautiful women in The Family. This also meant that he wanted me in the photo along with everyone else.

I didn't really care to be in the photo, because I just had a baby and was feeling self-conscious. I was nursing Stardust inside the house when a member came running in looking for me. They said that Father was waiting for me and refused to take the photo until I was there—and that I was holding up everything. So I got Stardust situated and put her to sleep, and then ran out to be in the photo. This is why I'm on the far left end and disheveled.

The band performed free shows all over the Los Angeles area at high schools, colleges, and parks. We would all pile into the blue and white vans, following Father in his Rolls Royce, to our destinations. I was scared to go to these events—thinking that I might be noticed—so I blended in with the Family members to the best of my ability. I was praying that nobody would recognize me. I didn't want to get dragged back into the Halfway House.

Surprisingly, Yahowah didn't seem phased by it—here we were at these events, with 140 Family members, many young mothers with babies, some of them his wives. He wasn't exactly keeping our lifestyle a secret.

A memorable performance was the band's gig at Beverly Hills High School. In a way, this was my alma mater, as I'd gone to Beverly Hills High for about three months—because I was ditching Fairfax High too much, so the Principal "re-assigned me" as a "punishment." Now here I was, a few years later, a young mother and part of a growing family. Looking around at the faces of the current Beverly High students, I wondered if this is what my life would have been like if I'd never left home and joined The Family. It was incredibly embarrassing, and I prayed that no one there recognized me. Other than that, I thought it was amazing that Yahowah went there and played music for these kids.

Visualize the scene—beautiful women with long flowing hair, wearing white sexy dresses, like goddesses—flourished with silver, turquoise, and jade jewelry. Men wearing robes, with long hair and beards, and sashes around their waists. Most of us were anywhere from 15 years to 30 years old. There were also several children in The Family. In the center of it all, this big huge man who looked like God or Jesus.

Yahowah addressed the crowd: "This is all improvisation, you know. Everything you will hear here, we are doing it for you. We have not rehearsed a thing. We never know what we're going to get into. We live in the eternal now. When we get there, somehow it always happens, man. It's a new sound, see? You're going to hear, at the same time, believe it or not, what we hear. And together, if we can cross that barrier of the eternal now space, and have some kind of communication in this place, I think, children, you're going to get off. I ain't going to lay no trip on your head—don't worry, babies. No, I'm just going to speak wisdom to you. For I am known as Wisdom and Love. I am the Father you all wanted and never thought you had—*but you do have.*"

Talk of the Town

Jim Baker's son, Bart, invited his dad to come see him perform a gymnastics routine at Highland Hall High School in Northridge. We all caravanned in the Rolls Royce and the blue and white vans to see the performance. I was there with Stardust and lots of beautiful young women and men with long hair and beards, all dressed in white. We arrived at the school and Father emerged from the Rolls Royce, surrounded by his women. At the time, he was with Ahom and Makushla.

We all followed him, at least 100 of us, many with babies in arms, walking with confidence and light, to a big outdoor lawn area overlooking the gymnastics setup. From there we could see the parallel bars, uneven bars, and the horse set up on the field, as well as the shocked looks on the faces of the spectators: other kids' parents, students, and teachers who were sitting, jaws-agape, in the bleachers.

First Father sat down, then we all sat down, cross-legged and quiet. Bart came running over to Father and they embraced in a big hug. All eyes focused on Bart, who had told Father exactly what time he was performing. A few minutes later, Bart performed his routine on the parallel bars. Something like 45 seconds. We all clapped.

Father called out to Bart: "Son, that was really good. Do you have anything else to show us?"

Bart responded, "No, that was it."

With that, Father stood up and lifted both of his arms. In unison, every Family member stood, and we then followed Father out to the waiting Rolls and VW caravan, and were gone within a matter of minutes. According to Bart, this event would be the talk of the school for weeks and months to come.

She's Not Your Woman

Things got interesting at The Father House. Father decided to take on a few more women and he let the men have more than one woman. This was completely different from the concept of "there's one woman to one man"—a quote from the book *Liberation* written by Jim Baker. Commandment VI: "The Man and his Woman are One, let nothing separate them."

Now any of the men could take on another woman. I'm guessing Father felt since he did this, then he should let his sons do the same thing. It was chaos and an exciting change at the same time. Not sure if I felt this was a good idea. It caused a lot of jealousy among the women.

At The Father House, after I already had Stardust, Father summoned me and Starman up to his bedroom to talk to us. This wasn't uncommon. After we sat down together, Father spoke to Starman, referring to me, and said, "She's not your woman. She belongs to my son."

This was a mystery to me. Was he referring to his "Earthly" son, Bart? Or another of the Sons in the Family?

Starman stared straight ahead, detached, and did not show any emotion, which seemed strange to me. I was embarrassed by his remark. I was in love with Starman at the time and this was the furthest thing from my mind. I wasn't sure where this came from, since Bart wasn't even in The Family.

At the time, I didn't think too much about it. Now looking back, Father saw something in the future that I did not. Bart and I were together a long time ago when I was twelve years old. But now I was a woman with a young child in a relationship with Starman. I was happy being with him and Stardust.

When Stardust was about one month old, Bart came to the Father House to visit his dad and to see me. Bart met Stardust there for the first time. In the context of the Father House, Bart was like a Piscean from out in the world, and I didn't relate to him at the time. I did let Bart hold Stardust and I think he was blown away that I had a baby.

Every time I saw Bart I got this pit in my stomach. I knew I still had feelings for him but we were in different worlds. He was a Piscean living in the Maya (terminology we used to refer to 'conventional society' out in the world–outside of The Source Family) with his mom and going to high school, like a normal teenager. I had a baby and was a loyal member of The Source Family with his dad as the leader of the commune. It couldn't have been more strange to see Bart. My focus was being the best disciple in the spiritual world.

At the Father House we had many visitors who came to experience our morning meditation, including Yogi Bhajan (Jim's mentor), Elaine Baker, Beau Baker (Bart's older brother), and Michael (Jim Baker's son from Ohio). One morning we were visited by Steve Allen, the creator and host of *The Tonight Show*. Steve knew Jim for years, from Jim's days as a restaurateur, and Steve knew how far out he was. Steve's son Logic Israel was (briefly) in The Family.

Labor Pains

All of our children were born at home, naturally—without medications or "modern medical technology." This was very unusual in the seventies. Most normal people gave birth to babies in proper hospitals. Not us. Father's philosophy was that children would be born at home, and should be brought into the world in a peaceful manner, with chanting, candles, and soft, spiritual music. A calm atmosphere to welcome them into the world.

In The Family we also didn't have traditional schooling—the children were free spirits. Their experiences in The Family were their "classroom" where they learned life skills—how to meditate, how to chant, and proper nutrition. At this time, I didn't mind, because my baby was an infant. Actually I didn't even think about school.

Ahom (Robin), who most Family members called Mother, had her baby in August 1974. This was Father's first of all his biological children born in The Family. I was at Ahom's birth, and Tau was delivered in Father's bedroom. There were just a few of us there. Father delivered his baby girl. Ahom had some complications, but Tau was born very healthy, and it was a joyous day.

In September, my close sister Anastasia was expecting her baby with Octavius, the drummer in the band. Soon after Libra was born, Ananstasia wasn't feeling well. Anastasia developed a staph infection on her breast and it spread to the baby. The situation was looking bad and we (Octavius—father of the baby, me, and Stardust) broke the rules and took Anastasia to the hospital. This was completely against Father's teachings. But our instincts kicked in and we had to do it. If we hadn't, then both mother and baby would have died.

After Anastasia went to the hospital with Octavius, I left and went back to The Father House. Later I learned that the hospital staff started asking Anastasia and Octavius questions about their living environment. The hospital authorities were startled by their answers about The Source Family commune, and started getting social services involved.

This intrusion from the authorities caused a crisis and prompted Father to move fast to protect the other underage mothers, and young women in The Family. This situation was unbeknownst to all of us at the time, because Father kept it all private from us. Lovely—one of the underage women who was around my age—was taken away by her father, Andre Previn, the famous music conductor. He shipped her off to a boarding school in Europe where she would finish her high school.

Then one day during morning meditation, Yahowah, in a matter of five minutes, decided that all of the mothers, children, and underage women needed to move to Hawaii—escorted by a few of the men. Right away. He said, "We are all going to Molokai. Find the land."

Every single minute of being in The Family was a constant roller-coaster. On a daily basis I was unsure of what would happen next. I felt that my life was in constant flux. All Father had to do was open his mouth and say, "I want to go to Molokai," and it became an overwhelming reality. "So Mote It Be," as Father was often to say (quoting the Freemasons)—or "So May It Be." Let it happen.

Everyone hung on his every word—including me. It was the word of God. I found it hard to say "no" to him. I felt Yahowah was invincible. The women built up Father's ego—they kept telling him that he was God, and perhaps he started to believe it.

That's when I learned that we were going back to Hawaii. And I actually felt comfortable about it, because I was afraid of staying in Los Angeles—where the authorities might find me and drag me back into "the system."

Why were we leaving the Father House for Molokai? At the time, nobody knew the reason why we were moving. Maybe some could guess or speculate about the reason. It was true that we needed to find a new place to live where we could practice our lifestyle and beliefs. We were looking for land to live our lives in peace without any trouble.

I found out later that the Feds and police were investigating Father for having underage girls there and "allegedly" having sex with them. Underage girls were running away from home. Young children in The Family were not going to school. Babies were being born "naturally" at home—without midwives or nurses. This was all illegal, and social workers and parents were being alerted.

Father wanted to make sure we were all safe from any legal matters. It was time to leave LA. Meanwhile he would begin the process of selling The Source Restaurant. This would take time. It would not be a completed sale—meaning there would be a transition period of time where some people had to stay on with the new owners of The Source.

First, Father sent most of the women, mothers with babies and children, and some of the men to Molokai, with the belief that we were going to find land and build a house and a farm, and we were going to live in a commune. We had barely any material possessions, so there wasn't much to pack. We put everything in cardboard boxes, loaded them into our vans, and shipped it all over to Molokai.

The about The Source (which included almost everyone there, except the babies), who were older than me, were like my parents. I was only 17 years old, and not really told or kept in the loop about anything that was going on. And if I asked, I was told that I was on an ego trip and not to worry. We all truly believed in what we were doing. We were not captive. Anyone could leave at any time. This was not the family that we were born into—it was The Family we chose to have.

Stardust and friend wearing matching dresses
I made for them

Chapter 6

ISLAND FEVER

Women and Children First

Molokai is a virgin island, very lush, and not as populated as the rest of the Hawaiian islands. We thought that we could find a new place to live and set up our lives our way. I envisioned a quiet lifestyle and warm weather beneath a tropical sun surrounded by waterfalls and rainbows. A place that we could call home.

Yahowah did not go to Molokai, just the women and children, and some of the men. Yahowah was still at The Father House. Starman stayed behind too to help get The Source Restaurant ready to sell.

We all flew in at different intervals from LA to Oahu, where we would all congregate and wait for each other's flights to come in. In Oahu airport, as we waited for hours, all day, for everyone else to arrive, lots of the moms like me were whipping out boobs to nurse babies and infants. People would stare at us, but we weren't shy in the least about nursing—anywhere, anytime. From Oahu we took Aloha Airlines, one of the smaller airlines, to Molokai. There were only two different flights there per day. By the time we got there, it was later in the day, but still light out.

We drove into Molokai in a caravan of rented vans (not the blue and white vans from LA) and we made our way through the town. This island looked very different from the other islands. My initial impression was that it was like driving through a third-world country. It was primitive and I didn't see any tourists there. We were aware that the island was recently the location of a leper colony, which was slightly unsettling.

It was only the local Hawaiians that seemed to live on this island. Houses looked like funky shacks and old cars were strewn about everywhere parked on lawns. Stray dogs were wandering around. I was blown away. The Hawaiians were just hanging out on their porches, staring at us and wondering who we were.

Where the heck were we going? I was once again unaware of the logistics of how the elders found us a place to live, and was praying, with complete faith, that it would be a good decision. I seriously didn't have to worry about anything.

We drove about an hour from the airport to our destination. Once we got outside of the town, we could see the lush landscape and gorgeous waterfalls as we cruised up the coast. At last we came to a big house (don't know whose house) across the street from the beach. It was a two-story house with a big lawn out front, and it had plenty of room for all (fifty?) of us. Everybody found their own space and we slept on the floor. We each had a cardboard box with our belongings.

Taking care of our babies was the most important job. Much of this involved washing diapers. In Molokai, we didn't have any washing machines, so it was a constant chore to clean our dozen cloth diapers that we each had. (We didn't use disposable diapers, since they were unnatural.) We all had a stack of our own diapers, which we would safety-pin on the babies. I always carried Stardust's baby stuff on me at all times—I had a bag with all her cloth diapers. We had plastic cover-ups, which we put over the diapers, and were supposed to limit any leakage—however they were barely effective.

We would have to wash the diapers by hand—first rinsing them with a hose outside, to get rid of the soil, then bringing the soaking wet smelly diapers into a large metal pot with boiling water—then mix in cold water and a natural laundry detergent, stirring them by hand. My hands were shriveled all the time. Now that's dedication. Then we would take the diapers outside to hang dry them on the clothesline. They would then become stiff and it was challenging to put a stiff dry diaper on a baby.

I basically cleaned diapers and our clothes all day long. Half the time, we would wash our clothes on rocks. I felt like I was living in another century. It was so primitive and I secretly dreamt of having a washer and a dryer.

Paradise Unravels

At first, I was totally on board with being in Molokai and ok with it. I had the security of all the women who were with me. No matter where I went, I felt pretty secure. I was young enough that I didn't have to make any major decisions.

And then the staph infections came, and paradise started to unravel. Staph infected all the babies and mothers—a rash on the skin that spreads throughout the body, highly contagious. I believe that everyone got staph infections from the ocean water. At the time I had no idea how severe staph could be (later on,

I learned that if it goes into your bloodstream, you can die from it). The infection was so intense that some of the members left Molokai—and left The Family altogether, and went to see a doctor—totally against the Family teachings.

Pretty much the whole time in Molokai we all had staph. I was grateful to only get the infection on my arms, although they were totally covered in staph. Really gnarly open sores. It was painful to have all these open wounds on our bodies. I felt so ugly having the sores all over. It was a challenging time for all of us. My biggest concern was taking care of my child. Stardust had staph everywhere on her body, on her head and all over her legs and arms.

It was very difficult to get rid of the staph infections. Especially in a commune in close quarters, it was terribly contagious. However we did cure most people from the infection—it just took a long while. Waterfall taught us how to make natural remedies—he knew so much about illnesses treated with herbs. Everything we did in The Family was always treated naturally.

Waterfall had Bo, the herb man in The Family, ship over the medicinal herbs to help the healing process. We made an herbal paste of goldenseal and echinacea compresses, which we made fresh everyday. We would make the paste in a bowl with goldenseal and echinacea, then soak the cloth in the bowl, then I would put the paste on the staph infection. I had to put the paste all over Stardust's body. She was so uncomfortable and irritable. And so was I.

The sores were often big open wounds. We didn't have any medicine to ease the pain, like Advil or Tylenol. Stardust's only comfort was me holding her and rocking her to sleep. I was grateful to only get the infection on my arms. I kept goldenseal patches on her open wounds around the clock to make sure that she healed naturally.

Back to Maui

After this episode, I wanted to get off of Molokai as quickly as possible. There was nothing about it that I liked. Spending all day boiling diapers and washing clothes was getting old. The mothers talked amongst each other and generally agreed that this didn't seem like the best place to set up and raise our children.

We heard from Family members in LA that—in another morning meditation—Father Yahowah decided that Molokai was not the place we were going to have our Family. We would all be moving together to Maui. This was another 10-minute decision, from what I understand. But in my eyes, this was a good decision. We were all ready to go.

Everyone who was in Molokai would leave for Maui and reunite with most of the men. Yahowah was still in LA. We all left Molokai and flew to Maui to look for a place to live. Some of the elders found a few houses on Baldwin Beach. From our house in Baldwin Beach, I could walk to Paia anytime (a funky little rustic beach community with lots of cafes and artsy stores and random hippies hanging around) and not have to ask for a ride. Baldwin Beach sometimes had rough waves and the sand was full of stickers that fell from the trees (watch your step!) Mostly we hung out at the beach with the babies and swam. There wasn't much else to do if you were a nursing mother. I cleaned the house and took care of Starman and Stardust.

One day Damian and Starman were sitting in Charlie's Restaurant in Paia and a man yelled out, "Does anyone know how to cook?" The man was Charlie, the owner, and he wanted a break from the restaurant.

Damian responded, "I do."

One thing led to another, and he asked Damian if he wanted to take it over. The name of the restaurant became "Goodies Bakery Cafe." Father had asked all the men to go and look for work, so this was perfect timing. All the men that were on the island from The Family ran the business and any women that didn't have a baby worked there too. It took a while to get it going, but they managed to start making some money.

Waterfall Whistles, Starman Reacts

Something dramatic happened in Maui between Starman, Waterfall, Stardust, and me that changed my feelings for Starman. The event that took place was never told to Father, because if it was, Starman would have been kicked out of The Family. I knew that I didn't want that to happen. Subconsciously that started a thought process for me to slowly slip away from my feelings for Starman.

As I was walking down the street in Paia with Starman and Stardust, suddenly there was the sound of a whistle. It was Waterfall whistling at me as he drove past us in the Goodies van. Starman (jealously?) reacted, maybe without thinking, and shoved me in a jealous nudge. Holding Stardust in my arms, I lost my balance and fell into a glass window of a vacant storefront. As I fell, fortunately I was able to protect her.

Waterfall got out of the car and quickly came over and helped

me up. He took a fist to Starman and knocked him down. This
was very uncharacteristic behavior for Waterfall. When Starman
stood up, Waterfall was screaming and yelling at him. Starman
was devastated and he was extremely apologetic. He genuinely
felt really bad. Waterfall picked me up and took the glass off of
me, handpicking all of the glass out of my arms. It wasn't in a lot
of places, but definitely I got cut. He left Starman there, and took
me and Stardust to the Goodies bakery kitchen, checking my
body for any more glass.

Fortunately, Yahowah wasn't there. He was still in LA. I
asked Waterfall to please not tell Yahowah. Yahowah was all
about being the perfect gentleman. This incident would not have
gone over well.

This was a pivotal moment. Starman was becoming controlling and possessive. I believe that Starman didn't mean to
shove me. It was an impulse. According to Damian (who told me
later), Starman's perception of our relationship was that "I had
a 'high-school crush' on him." Yeah, right. I don't do well with
being possessed and controlled.

I started to lose my interest in him slowly over that year. It
got to the point where I didn't want to be with him at all. It was
difficult, because I am a very loyal person. He wasn't a bad guy,
but I couldn't help what I was feeling. This incident was a turning
point—the beginning of the end.

Early on in our relationship, I was ok with Starman being
seven years older than me. I looked up to him and I took really
good care of him. I respected my duties as an Angel. An Angel
means that you are the woman who serves your man and takes care
of him. A Mother Angel means that you take on the authority of

a mother role to your man, and take care of his needs. A Mother role means that you only take on the authority responsibilities of your man, and someone else does the Angel duties. I was clearly an Angel only to Starman. I served Starman the way Yahowah taught the women how to serve their men.

We were completely detached from modern society, and whatever feminist women's movement may have been going on back on the mainland. In The Source Family, relationships were the most important. We had our own philosophy about how a woman treats her man. Yahowah taught us to give up our egos and give without needing to receive—live selflessly and not expect anything in return. In other words, live without an ego. So we did our own thing. We lived by it. And we agreed. It was about both partners giving to each other in a relationship.

As a 17 year old, I did everything in my power to give myself to him completely. He was really good to me 99% of the time. Loving and kind. He was a great father and adored Stardust. I was trying to sort out my feelings. It was a very hard decision for me to sort out my feelings for him at my young age of 17. I felt like I was committed because we had a child together. I wanted to be a loving, kind, nourishing, hands-on kind of mother—unlike my own mother, who did none of those things when I was growing up. I felt that I should stick it out and make it work.

Even though we were there as a Family, we were individuals in our own world. Our teachings were not to get attached to anyone or anything. I was in a constant battle with myself to not get too closely attached to Starman. I felt like I was only there because of my daughter, Stardust. As The Family was evolving I was growing up and changing in a different direction. I would have never left The Family on my own (Where would I even go? Back to the Halfway House?), like some others who abruptly left when they didn't agree with what was going on.

The real reason that we were living in the Hawaiian Islands? Father said it was a safe place to weather the storm of nuclear war—that would occur in September of the year 2001. In that sense, we were in a Doomsday Cult, in that we were oftentimes delirious—sleep deprived, hungry, and living in fear of impending nuclear war. In retrospect, considering the catastrophic terrorist attacks of 9/11/2001—Yahowah's prediction was eerily accurate.

We all believed the word of Father that we needed a safe place. You might say that we were spiritually brainwashed. That is very possible. Regardless, it was a reality for us. Who is to say what is reality or what's not? It was our reality. I certainly can see how the outside world would see it as "we are living in a false dream state of consciousness." That will be determined in history whether or not to be true.

After a few months on Maui, it was time to move on again, in search of terra nova—somewhere with fewer people, where we could live in peace. Father told us to pack up as we were moving to the Garden Isle of Kauai. I didn't know why we were leaving Maui. Why would anyone leave Maui? Nobody told me. I could only guess that Father thought we would be safer in a quieter, more secluded environment. Maybe Kauai was the answer.

Father greets the morning sun in Maui

Chapter 7

UNWELCOME TO PARADISE

The Bad Hippies on the Beach

As soon as we arrived in Kauai in December of 1974, we walked off the plane and received horrible looks from the locals. We couldn't quite understand why they were reacting that way. After all, they didn't know us. We later found out that we were being mistaken for being "the bad hippies on the beach," who were drugged out, running around naked, and leaving trash and pollution everywhere. They were sleeping on the beach, virtually homeless, and committing crimes, causing a major public nuisance.

Unfortunately we were getting lumped in with the wrong crowd, even though we were nothing like them. The men in The Family had long hair and beards, and because of the way we were dressed, the locals put us in that category. Wherever we went in Kauai, we got these shady looks. Even though I was secure within The Family people, I felt uneasy.

Kauai was a very wet experience—it's one of the wettest spots on earth. It rained all the time. Because of that, when the sun came out, there were constantly lots of rainbows. Sometimes two or three rainbows at a time. Some rainbows were in circles and some had three or four arches at a time. So many rainbows every day.

It was as close to paradise as one could imagine—lush, green and fragrant. The smell of the island was like perfume, plumeria and tuberose. Kauai was colder than the other islands. So pretty and beautiful—waterfalls everywhere and green vines growing with flowers that I'd never seen before. We would go hiking to the waterfalls, and swim in the water pools. One of our special hikes was going to the Sleeping Giant Trail, a famous mountain that looks like a sleeping giant. Some called it The Grand Canyon of Hawaii.

Soon a shipping container from LA arrived in Kauai with all of our stuff—beddings, material to make clothes, all the sewing equipment. We had filled up two of our vans to the brim with as much as we could. It felt so good to get all of our stuff, and made us feel more like we were at home.

The Family elders found us a property on a ranch in Kapa'a on 13 acres, with a main house and five little houses. Our new house was walking distance to the beach, hiking and waterfalls. It was perfect for us and housed everyone comfortably. In the main house, Father, Makushla, Ahom and his Council Women lived. We had our morning meditations there. It was primitive living for us. 20-25 people in the main house. The rest of the 100 people were living outside on the property in huts or tents. At least in Kauai we had a kitchen, washing machines and bathrooms, although some of the bathrooms were outhouses.

I lived in a hut (tiny cottages without bathrooms or kitchens) with Starman, Stardust and Aura. (That's around the time when Aura came into the picture—Starman's new (second) woman).

Aura arrived in The Family in June 1974 (when we were in The Father House) and at first, she was with Damian. And then, a couple months later, she was with Starman when I was in Molokai. Aura was only in The Family for one year—she came much later into The Family than me. Father always was looking for more people to join us and be saved from the Piscean world.

Aura was quiet and withdrawn, unlike me and Starman, who were both more animated and social. She was around the same age as Starman, about seven years older than me, but I had been with Starman for a longer time, so we had more of a bond and we were closer, with some balance of authority in the relationship.

Aura was sensitive to my space with Starman. She wasn't competitive (at least, I didn't think so). She really loved him, maybe a lot more than me. I didn't feel bad about it. Almost everyone was having more than one woman. It was the thing to do. All three of us got along really well. And Aura got pregnant in Kauai.

At the hut, we had makeshift showers with a hose. The water was always freezing cold. (I didn't have a hot shower for five years, so I didn't know what I was missing.) Father referred to this as a "military shower"—you had to wash your hair and important private body parts, and get to the point—and be done in less than five minutes.

The shock of the cold water made your body shiver and your kundalini rise, releasing energy. Nobody complained, because this is what we signed up for. This is what we were used to. Spiritual Bootcamp. "Change is the only constant thing in the universe," as Father often would say.

After going through this, my body adapted to ice cold water, and nothing cold would ever bother me again. I could jump into a cold river and be completely fine. (However, today I prefer hot water.)

Only the main house had a kitchen and bathrooms. The smaller houses did not have restrooms. All the bathrooms (outhouses) and showers were outside, down a pathway, not close to us at all. It was always wet and rainy, and we mostly walked barefoot. I barely wore shoes or sandals for almost the whole time in Hawaii.

In order to get to the outhouses (bathrooms) at night, we would have to walk outside in the dark, with no lights. We were at the mercy of "feeling it." At night and after a rain, the pathways on our property were inundated with big fat frogs (cane toads). They were a plant-like green color, with big bulging eyes. If I had to go to the bathroom at night, I would walk barefoot in the dark on the pathway to the outhouse and sometimes accidentally step on the frogs. Squishy and gooey and gross. There was no way around it.

Every morning when the sun came up, you could see all the dead frogs from people stepping on them. Some of the Sons would go and clean up all the dead frogs on the pathways after morning meditation. Ever since this time, I've developed a strong personal dislike for frogs.

That's when we started having mud-baths. Father thought the very rich soil in Hawaii would be healing. So we dug bath-sized places into the ground and literally took mud baths to purify the toxins and get them out of our bodies. This became a common practice when we were in Kauai.

Morning Glory

Many of the sermons at morning class were somewhat comical. Like when Yahowah taught us how to use toilet paper. He would give a sermon on how to fold the toilet paper. How much paper you use. Two pieces of paper. How you should wipe from the front to the back. This would always cause lots of laughter. Of course his women would support him to the fullest with shews and awes. Whatever he said—it was the word of God. It seemed like we were on his journey, his ride and path. We were there for support. This was his movie and we all played supporting roles.

Yahowah would often talk about silly things and it would cause laughter, that was much needed comic relief. Most of the sermons were esoteric and hard to understand. Even if I wasn't exactly sure if I was hearing him right, somehow I always did understand with my intellect.

Yahowah was always seizing every opportunity to teach us. This always happened after we meditated, chanted, did hatha yoga breathing and smoked a puff of the sacred herb (marijauna). By the time meditation was over we were pretty stoned and high, like sponges ready to absorb whatever was said.

For morning meditations, we would all congregate in the main house at 4 a.m. into the huge living room and have our class. A typical morning meditation involves passing around the sacred herb, drinking our special coffee, sitting in a lotus position on a folded blanket, chanting like angels, waiting for Yahowah to come and guide us in meditation. It was easy for me to get into a deep place, especially after smoking one hit of sacred herb.

The hatha breathing exercises would put me into a higher

place. I felt so light and pure after hatha yoga. After about an hour of sitting in a lotus position my legs and knees started to get painful. Father always said that you can turn pain into pleasure. I believed this to be true, however I'm not sure I ever felt the pleasure. We would typically sit for two hours.

It was amazing to see that Father could sit in a full lotus for over two hours without ever stretching. I was in awe of his flexible ability. When he spoke I listened intently to his every word. I felt that he had knowledge and there were things I needed to learn from him. I'm not sure if I was brainwashed or just an extremely devoted disciple. My love for him was intense, like a father.

After about an hour of meditation and chanting, Yahowah would give a sermon. It was always different. To me, this was a highlight of my experience in The Source Family. It was a great way to start the day. He would always add in some stories of his past. He often would say: "All truths are half truths." Meaning that you could embellish your story—and make it so.

And then after the morning meditation everybody would disperse and do their duties—go to work, go to the beach, mud bath, go on a hike, etc. Clean the house and take care of the children and babies. This was how our Family life played out daily. Sometimes we would go on excursions to Black Sands Beach to collect Puka Shells to make necklaces and anklets. It was Father's dream to have all the women stay home and all the men go to work and earn money to support The Family.

After our chores were done, Anastasia, Azure, and I would go hike to the waterfalls with our babies. We literally carried our babies and our bags and walked for miles. The hike was always muddy and slippery. We enjoyed swimming in the fresh crisp water. It was always hot and humid so this was a welcome swim. A rainbow would appear almost daily and sometimes a double rainbow. I've never seen so many different rainbows—doubles, triples, and circles.

The 12 Council Women

Back when we were living in the Father House in Nichols Canyon, Los Angeles, Yahowah convened a Council of 12 women—each of them had a specific job to do for Yahowah and The Family. After all the traveling and moving around, the Council seemed to be more serious once we settled in Kauai.

Among the most important players on the Council, who were all totally devoted to Yahowah, were Makushla—who Yahowah called his Mother, Ahom—who the Family called their Mother and who was Yahowah's legal wife and his Mother Angel, and Prism—who Yahowah called his Angel.

The rest of the Council Women seemed to play different roles for Yahowah. The Council Women were completely devoted to the cause—however it was never specifically decided about what their roles were. I wasn't always clear on who did what, but they were clear amongst each other. It looked to me like the Council Women took it upon themselves to take care of Yahowah's needs.

Makushla was with Yahowah (aka her "Kitty") all the time. He always wanted her by his side. It was obvious that he was very much in love with Makushla. She was well respected amongst all of us. Makushla was always loving and kind. I felt comfortable being around her. The love that they shared was inspiring. She seemed to be the most unattached of his women, and yet the most demanded from him.

Paralda was the chef to Yahowah. She was self-confessed not the greatest cook, and mainly prepared two items—vegetable soup with cottage cheese, and broccoli with melted cheese. It was also her job to massage some of the Council Women, including Mother Ahom.

Each of the Council Women represented the 12 Zodiac astrological signs—and they brought different personalities and energies to the relationship. The Council Women were treated well and respected amongst the members of The Source Family, and they made most of the decisions in the running of the household.

Some of the The Council Women members would change over time. They thought that it was a high honor to be one of the 12 Council Women—but I'm not so sure about that. How does one man satisfy 12 women (sexually, or otherwise) and keep them all happy? In reality, some of the Council Women had relationships with other men in The Family—which made this even more of a questionable arrangement. The women seemed so devoted to Yahowah, yet they sought out other companionship.

I experienced a lot of drama amongst these 12 women. They didn't always agree amongst themselves on all Family matters. They seemed to fight a lot and compete over who would be favored and who would have sex with Father. There was some jealousy, understandably, but at the same time, there was a sisterhood about them. They were in a position of authority, and it was a tough position to be in.

Going Coconuts

In Kauai, our diet was basically the indigenous foods of the island—avocados, mangos, pineapple, bananas, papayas, macadamia nuts, and sometimes, on occasion, fish. We added brown rice as a staple to our diet. Who knows what Yahowah and the Council Women were eating in the main house? That's a debate I often wondered about.

The food trip got really boring after a while. I was so thin (maybe 110 pounds? We didn't have a scale, so who knew?) and hungry most of the time. I would talk about food and dream of what I would eat if I could have anything I wanted. Mostly I just craved dairy products, dates, and ice cream. Often we would resort to finding nuts grown on the island. Macadamia nuts grew everywhere. Anastasia was good at cracking them. So was Azure. To crack a nut, I would find a strong rock, put the nut on the ground and pound on it until it cracked open. This usually took about two to three minutes to crack per nut. It helped to pass the time.

The men would pick pineapples in the fields and climb up trees for coconuts. We would use the coconuts to make coconut water—and to make all sorts of things, and eat the meat inside the coconut. The color of the coconut would tell you what type of meat you would get. Green (young) coconut meant soft meat, but the juice was good. If it was green and brown, it would be medium—crunchy. If it was all brown and hairy—it was hard meat, but the juice was sweetest.

I would drink the juice right out of the coconut. I made flatbread with seeds and nuts—gluten free, no flour. At this time, we were vegan, and therefore we didn't have any dairy products. No sugar was allowed (ever, during the entire time), but we were allowed to have (technically non-vegan) natural, unfiltered honey.

Fresh fish was added to our diet when Yahowah told the men to go out and buy a boat. The men found a boat for sale and it was called the Shime Maru. They bought it from a fisherman, and it came with a small propeller plane to scout fish. Sunflower and a few other brothers happened to have pilot's licenses. Starman was one of the fishermen on the boat.

They caught lots of fish for The Family—but they couldn't sell the fish to any of the businesses on the island. We were not locals, and no one would buy from us. I know this was challenging to the men—they had worked so hard to catch the fish and sell them—it was hoped to be another source of income for us.

Caught in a Riptide

I love the water, the ocean, the waves. I was always the first to go out there, and the last to come back. I always loved swimming way out past the waves like a mermaid. I was so fearless those days. Some days the waves were so big we couldn't swim. The beach was close by and in walking distance. Swimming in the ocean was our most stable exercise.

The ocean was rough in Kauai and sometimes dangerous. One day we all went to the beach for a swim. Some of us, including me, got stuck in a riptide. There weren't any lifeguards and the current was taking us way out into the ocean. There were fifteen members stuck in the current that day.

Someone was thinking fast and orchestrated the members to hold hands all the way onto the beach and into the ocean to rescue the members stuck out. It took about twenty five Family members to reach us out there. It was one of the scariest times I had in the ocean. Once they pulled us back onto the beach I was so out of breath and exhausted from fighting the undertow. I thought it was so smart for that member to think of this and save the day.

Local Tension

We also played music during this time—the band practiced their music at all hours. I loved when the music would play and I could hear it while I walked around the property. I particularly liked the folk songs by Ahom, Aladdin and Gjin. But the music was loud, and the neighbors could hear it too. And they started to complain.

Kauai was a beautiful place, but we were not wanted. As time went on, we couldn't go too many places. One day a couple women were walking down the driveway at the end of the property, when they heard gunshots. They ran back to the house and told Yahowah, who was livid.

Then the locals started harassing us with firecrackers and guns, making us feel very unwelcome. The message was clear: "You don't belong here." That was why we had to defend ourselves.

After the gunshots were fired, we armed up. First, we got our hands on a .45 pistol. (Alex—Zinaru's gun.) The men took turns on lookout in a watch tower. This didn't actually make us feel safe—in fact, it had the opposite effect. It seemed that there was violent energy in Kauai everywhere. I didn't want to go any-where. I didn't feel safe.

Yahowah decided to go on a world tour to find a new home for us all to live together. Then he left to go to Nepal (when the Family was in Kauai). He wanted to see if we should move to India. He took Makushla and a couple of men and women with him. It was strange to have Yahowah going to India during this weird, insecure time in Kauai. I couldn't imagine moving all the way to India with everybody—and actually being successful. The India trip turned out to be more of an adventure, versus a scouting out of new locations.

Yahowah, in his white shawl with long hair, looked like a spiritual leader. People were following him everywhere. I later found out that, while on tour, Father was eating meat, smoking cigarettes—doing the opposite of what he taught us in The Fam-ily (per Damian, who was there and later told me about it). Of course, no one in The Family knew about this.

Yahowah's world tour began in early March 1975 and he went to Thailand, India, Nepal, Bhutan, Egypt (twice to the Pyramids), and several countries in Europe (Greece, Denmark, Germany, and England), Canada, and the Pacific Northwest. At the time, I was so focused on my relationship and baby, and surviving in The Family, that I didn't think too much about Yahowah being gone on this world tour.

Meanwhile, the Kauai government literally wanted to pay for us to leave the island. Yahowah thought that we would blend in better in San Francisco. He wanted us to be far enough away from LA, where the authorities might find me and the other underage kids.

When we were moving from Kauai to San Francisco, I had no feelings about it. I was at the mercy of whatever Yahowah wanted us to do. "Get on board and don't have an ego about it." It was a very insecure time for all of us. It was a definite test about who could handle the change, and who could not. "Everything is a test. Let's see if you pass." There was no plan. Everything was living in the eternal now.

Walking with Father in Kauai (me near top left corner)

Chapter 8

THE STREETS OF SAN FRANCISCO

Homeless: 30 Days of Hell

Spring 1975

Why go to San Francisco? This was not a well-thought-out plan. "Let's pack up all of our vans and go . . . " We thought SF might be a place with other like-minded people—the music was also a major reason. But by now, we didn't have that much money and everyone was trying to scramble money to get airplane tickets. My airplane ticket was bought by Starman's father. We were headed back to the mainland.

When we all arrived in San Francisco, we were totally unprepared for the freezing weather. I wore a long cotton dress and flip-flops (no jacket or sweater), and little Stardust was cold too, as much as I bundled her up like a mummy in her blanket. To make matters worse, we soon found out that we had no place to live. Somehow that part hadn't been planned out. So we lived on the streets and used the bathrooms in churches to wash our faces and freshen up. We literally lived out of a box with our babies and children. I had never felt so insecure before. I never felt more anxiety than I did about being homeless. Somehow we must have eaten, but all I can remember is constantly feeling hungry.

It was a very tough time in the commune. Many Family members couldn't take being homeless and living in the streets, or churches, or temporarily in other peoples' homes. It was too much for them to handle. Many Family members left during the San Francisco period. There was a growing feeling of disillusionment.

This was a test that I could have done without. I was numb, scared, and confused. I wasn't sure where Yahowah was staying, but I don't remember him or his wives sleeping in the street, like the rest of us. Later I found out that they were all staying in a hotel.

It made me feel inferior and vulnerable. Like I wasn't going to be treated as well. I had never noticed that before. I started to have doubts I was in the right place. I seriously thought about leaving The Family with Starman—for a nanosecond. I just didn't have the strength to leave. I was 17 and I was still a fugitive from the courts. Being a young mother was always challenging for me. Members didn't take me seriously. My voice would not have been heard. I felt stuck and decided to stay in The Family, praying that we would find a home soon.

Things started looking even more grim when one of my closest sisters, White Cloud, had to give birth to her baby boy, named Thunder, in a church. She was such a trooper. White Cloud was with Rhythm, who (unsurprisingly) was in the band. We were close in age and I was blown away at what she had to go through.

We then found temporary refuge at the Mill Valley home of Astral (a Council Woman)—whose parents were out of town.

After a few nights there, neighbors called the cops and we got kicked out. Next we stayed a few nights at Wheeler Ranch in Sonoma as Yahowah and the elders plotted our next move.

The Atherton Mansion

I prayed every day that we would overcome this test and find a place to live. Thank God that my prayers were answered, about thirty days later. Some of the Family members found the Atherton Mansion, a huge house (35 rooms) with many bedrooms and floors. I later learned that it was Electricity who found the house—he knew the area, because he had lived there before. He brought Father with him to scout the location, breaking open a back door to get inside. Father walked inside, looked around, and said, "Get me this house—I want it."

The house was in the heart of San Francisco (not to be confused with the city of Atherton, which was about 25 miles to the south), within walking distance of many parts of the city. However, the house was allegedly haunted and smelled like cat piss everywhere (as the prior occupant Carrie Rousseau kept over 50 felines). We went in and we cleaned it from top to bottom, and it never looked so good. We even created a classroom for the kids in the basement. We made it work.

Even as we settled into our new home, I was feeling very insecure and having doubts about my relationship with Starman. I wasn't sure he would take care of me and Stardust. I questioned the relationship and started keeping a distance from him.

Meanwhile, after morning meditations Father would go up to his room and many of the women would follow him, hoping to be invited in for Dhyanism. Dhyanism was our ancient sexual practice in The Family that was done regularly to gain strength of your inner forces—it was a spiritual sexual act, supposedly done as a sacred ceremony for a higher consciousness. It seemed everything we did had a spiritual meaning behind it. We always had a private space for this practice to take place. With so many people around living in tight quarters, this was necessary.

During Dhyanism sex, basically the man holds his seed (does not orgasm)—so the woman is allowed to oragasm, but not the man. It was Father's belief that the only time a man would release his seed was in order to procreate a child. Otherwise, you could do Dhyanism as much as you want. And for some people, that was a lot. (Is that what really happened throughout The Family? I'm not really sure if that's the way it came down—there were lots of pregnancies).

Standing My Ground

One day after morning meditation, all of the women and I followed Father Yahowah back to his room. I was wearing this long brown velvet dress with buttons going all the way down. It was very sexy and flattering on me. I may have looked a little older than I was, which was 17. I think I looked like I was twenty years old. I'm not sure if this had an effect on Yahowah—because, out of nowhere, Father asked me into his bedroom.

I wasn't sure why this time Father chose me, but I decided to join him. I walked into the dark room—candles lit, incense burning, set up for a romantic encounter. I wasn't sure exactly what was going to happen, but I had an idea. Makushla was in the room too, lying on a bed made of futons, velvet and silk pillows, and being supportive. For some reason this made me feel somewhat better.

Yahowah asked me to join him and sit on the bed—the Dhyanism area. So I did, reluctantly. I felt like I had to act interested in him sexually. It was supposed to be a spiritual experience, but I didn't feel that way. My heart started racing and I was thinking, "Oh my God, it's my turn—this is going to happen. I'm going to be one of the women who has Dhyanism with Father."

Father brought me close to him into his arms and had me sit on his lap. I realized that Yahowah was trying to get me to be one of his women.

Father asked me, "Do you want to have Dhyanism together?"

I was in an insecure place at the time and I thought about it. I started the motion of taking off my clothes and he did the same. But my mind was unraveling. I felt violated. I started to question—why was I there? Was this a safe place to be? I thought to myself, "Wait. Isn't Dhyanism supposed to be a spiritual experience to be shared with your man, your partner? I'm not sure I wanna do this."

In a way, I thought that I should be feeling excited about his invitation to be with him. Part of me felt like I was lucky and honored to be a part of this ritual. I knew what was to come, because the other women had talked to me about their encounters with Yahowah. But I also knew that many of the women that practiced Dhyanism with him were not his Council Women. They were just a one-time thing, and not meant to last. It wasn't a lifetime commitment.

This situation felt too much like an old man wanting to

have sex with a young, vulnerable teenager—far from a spiritual experience. Deep down inside, I just wanted to be Yahowah's daughter. Not his lover. I was a mess and I decided to decline to be one of his women. I felt awful that I didn't want to be with him. It didn't feel right to me. It was not my character. I didn't want that relationship with Father and I didn't even know that until I sat on his lap at that moment.

"No, I don't want to do Dhyanism with you, Father."

It wasn't easy for me to say no. I usually did not speak up and did not have a voice in The Family. I was quiet and reserved. But something inside me perhaps was so strong that I was able to stand my ground. There was my voice, finally.

Yahowah seemed surprised, and said to me: "Mushroom, I didn't know you had it in you."

He was taken back that I stood up for myself and said no. The good thing about the encounter is he was apologetic, gentle, gracious, and understanding—and he let me go. To me, Yahowah was always kind. He honored my decision and didn't try to change my mind.

I put my clothes back on and walked out of the bedroom, to where all the other women were there waiting their turn. They asked me what happened. I was numb and couldn't talk. I went straight to where Starman and Stardust were, embraced them both, and I held Stardust in my arms—still in disbelief of what had happened. I couldn't tell Starman about what happened. The reason why I didn't tell anybody is because people would think that I was crazy to not have sex with Yahowah and become one of his Council Women.

It just wasn't my spiritual path. That would've meant (to me) that I had to leave Starman and Stardust. I still loved Starman and couldn't imagine leaving him and Stardust. Even though I wasn't sure about us as a couple, I couldn't leave him. So I stayed and worked hard on trying to be a good woman. Father respected my decision and never approached me again. This changed my perspective of Yahowah—I started having serious doubts about who he really was. And this encounter has haunted me for close to fifty years.

Taking Care of Business

Father was frustrated and had doubts about the sons getting work to take care of the women and children. It was a constant issue that the men didn't get work. It was hard for the men to get jobs because of the way we all looked and dressed—the long hair and long beards, not to mention the long robes with sashes around the waist, and flip flops. There was a stigma that kept them from being hired.

Thus the men relied on Yahowah for everything—and they became like children. And it would be hard to leave his presence and go out in the Piscean world and work for Piscean people, even though they knew that they had to bring in money. Yahowah decided that he would take care of us women and children, meaning that he would stay at home with us and take care of us financially, while the Sons went out to find work.

It was hard for me to be an Angel and count on Starman to have his financial trip together. Starman kept saying that he wanted to leave. I told him that I wouldn't leave. In reality—I didn't have faith in him being responsible enough to take care of Stardust and me. But I think Aura would have gone with him in a second. I just didn't want to leave. I'm sure many members thought of leaving, and some did.

Life went on in San Francisco as best as we could. It was almost impossible for the men to find work. Father was disappointed in the men not bringing in money. At one point I thought the Family was going to disperse. It was nearly impossible for Father to take care of all of us by himself. Money was tight and the music business wasn't bringing in anything. I know some members left at this time and moved on. I know Father was frustrated with the lack of financial support from the men.

I started having anxiety attacks. At first, I didn't know what they were. I felt like I was losing control of my emotions. I had no idea what to do about my feelings.

When we first got into the mansion, it was so cold. None of us had the proper clothing. There was this one time that I was shaking uncontrollably. This was the first time this ever happened to me. Starman had to lie on top of me to get me warm and stop shaking. He had me take a hot bath to get in control of my body. I remember falling asleep in the bathtub with Stardust lying on my stomach because I was so exhausted from the homeless experience and being so cold. This was a huge wake-up call. I had to make a change.

Part of my anxiety might have been because I was a runaway. I was still on the run from the law. I had literally fled a Halfway House and was still a ward of the court. I was constantly looking over my shoulder. Now that we were back on the mainland, it seemed like I could be in more danger.

One afternoon I met Starman's dad in Lafayette Park, down

the block from the Atherton House. He was a really nice man. He saw Stardust for the first time. He was very loving towards her. I think that he was wondering if I was going to marry Starman. Starman's mom had died when he was in high school. Then his dad remarried, so he had a stepmother. They put him in military school when he was young. He had a brother and sister. It was so nice to meet his Father.

The focus of the time was the music. Jam sessions. Making records. Earlier in The Family, the music (to me) was so beautiful. In San Francisco, the sound took a decidedly psychedelic turn. Father would be playing the gong, loudly and off the beat, the band trying hard to follow his lead. If you were in the band— you were happening. The music was like rap or spiritual talk. Yahowah thought that through the music he could reach out to people in a spiritual way to come join our Family. From my perspective, it was all becoming a big ego trip and moving away from spirituality.

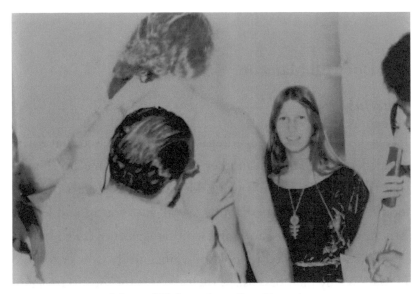

*Me and Yahowah in San Francisco
at the Atherton Mansion*

Chapter 9

THE BIG ISLAND

The Doc Hill Mansion

June-July 1975

It was during a morning meditation in San Francisco that Father decided to give Hawaii another chance. This time he thought that the Big Island would work. He sent a crew over to Hilo to look for a house for The Family. We all just got up and left the Atherton Mansion in San Francisco that was once called home.

Now we all needed to look for money to fly us over to Hilo, Hawaii. Many members asked their parents for the airfare again. This wasn't the first time. I knew I couldn't ask my mom, so Starman and Aura had to get the money for all of us. We all flew over to Hilo in intervals once a house was secured. The house was called the Doc Hill Mansion.

I remember flying over there, just the four of us (Me, Stardust, Starman, and Aura). So this time, fewer people stared at us, like before, as if there was a flock of white dressed angels gliding through the airport.

The Doc Hill Mansion was right on the ocean in Hilo. It was a beautiful Hawaiian house full of trees and flowers. There was a big ballroom, with a fireplace, where we had our morning meditations. The house was two stories and there was also a guest house. I don't know how we all fit there, but somehow we did. Most of us slept on the floor with our mats and rolled them up in the morning. We were all used to cramped quarters. I slept in the guesthouse with most of the mothers and babies.

On the ocean side was a sprawling grass lawn with a lava rock wall. A step ladder led into the Pacific Ocean where we would go swimming in the gently flowing tides. Many times Father and the women would just hang out on the lawn with the babies and chill. I don't mean just his Council Women, I mean all the women in The Family. I loved hanging out with him and listening to his sermons—which were different every day. Swimming was a big activity to do as a group. Walking was another favorite exercise for Father.

Life in Hilo at the Doc Hill Mansion seemed calmer to me. After everything we had been through over the past year, this was a welcome reprieve. Father didn't want the women to work. He wanted them to stay focused on their children. The mothers and the babies were always put together somewhere in the house, away from the rest of The Family. And I was happy about this.

The men started finding work doing construction and carpentry to support us—anything that they could to earn money. It wasn't easy working in long white robes. So the men had to wear pants and shirts to fit in. Money was coming in finally. Some of the men started a bakery called Goodies—just like the place we'd had in Maui. We still had the fishing boat and the spotter plane. Some men climbed coconut trees for coconuts. Starman was one of the men to do this.

Conflicted

Starman was always working to help support Aura and me and Stardust. Aura was pregnant and her baby was due in September. I was growing apart from Starman and seeking other relationships. I was part in and part out of our relationship. I questioned often if I was still a devoted disciple to Father. I had just turned eighteen and was changing rapidly.

Even though it was common for the sons to have more than one wife, it never felt right. Some of the sons were single and many of them only kept one wife. It's not that I was jealous, it was more that I didn't feel this could last with Starman. I was growing up and my goals became different from his.

I was starting to dream about the future, beyond The Family—maybe going to college in Los Angeles, getting a degree, and creating a secure environment for Stardust. Maybe even (gasp) cut my hair, shave, wear makeup, put on jeans and a pair of boots, drive a car, make some money, be something. My other goal was to leave Starman, but remain friends with him and hope to have him in Stardust's life.

My head was spinning with strange thoughts and worries about where I was going. Some of the other men picked up on this and started to pursue me. One of them was Jupiter who just joined The Family and was a hang glider from Lanikai, Oahu. Jupiter and I became close and spent a lot of time together. He was much older than me but I liked being around him. I also hung out with a few other men, but no one I felt like being with romantically.

Stardust was always my main focus. I spent most of my time

taking care of her, and with the other mothers who had babies the same age as Stardust—Anastasia and Azure, with their babies Angel and Libra. They were my support system and we helped each other get through the daily struggles, like just taking a nap or having some private time with our men. I would watch their babies while they were otherwise occupied, or needed to clean up their space, or hang out with Father.

I didn't know much about their lives before The Family. No one even knew that I was a fugitive. Or that my mother lost her parental rights and I became a ward of the court. It's so interesting that we didn't talk about the past. Like it was washed away from our brains. I'm sure every single person in The Family had a story, but I wouldn't know.

Detective Tracks Me Down

One day I was off with Anastasia, Azure, and our babies having a picnic outside on the grass. Suddenly one of the Sisters came looking for me, yelling, "Mushroom! Yahowah wants to see you! And DON'T bring Stardust!"

I was intrigued. I left Stardust with my sisters and went inside to the big ballroom. There I saw Yahowah and a man dressed in Piscean plain clothes, with glasses, sitting there, holding a picture of me.

Yahowah introduced me: "This is Wendy Lenore Gossard." (He did not tell them my Family name—aka Mushroom). It felt so weird to hear my "former name" said out loud. I thought that I would never hear that name again.

The man was a detective from Los Angeles who had come

all the way here looking for me. He was most likely from the LA County Sheriff's Department, trying to locate all the runaway underage children.

The detective declared, "I'm here to find her and take her back to Los Angeles."

Right at this moment, my heart stopped. My brain went fuzzy and I lost my sense of hearing. And I got so scared with the thought of having to go back to LA with my child, that it left me in a state of shock.

Yahowah pointed out to the detective that I had just turned 18 a few weeks ago. And that I had a child. And that it was very unnecessary for him to arrest me. Yahowah was so convincing. After a long conversation, the detective, amazingly, agreed with him. And as the detective left . . . *I became FREE.*

It was a big pivotal moment for me, that I no longer had to worry about being arrested, taken back to LA, and facing the court system again. I felt that, at this time in my life, I started to mature and grow up, and think differently about my future.

I wonder if—during the time I was in The Family—and throughout all the difficulties that we faced—that I stayed, because I knew that if I left, I could be taken into custody and become a ward of the court again. And put into a Foster Home.

After the detective left, I jumped into Yahowah's arms and kissed him, thanking him from my deepest heart, that he had saved me—once again.

When I later went back to see Azure and Anastasia, they asked me what happened. I told them, "It was the past. And it's all good now." And they accepted that. Because we lived in the now. That's how seriously we took not talking about the past.

Nobody else knew what I went through. To this very day, no one knows about my court experience. Or my stay in a Halfway House, or hiding out in Idyllwild and staying with Yahowah's friends, and then escaping to Maui.

Black Monday

August 25, 1975

During our time in Hilo, Father seemed, to me, to be getting bored. He began saying that he'd taught us everything he knows and it was time for him to move on. And that he wasn't God, he was just a man. Even though he said it, I didn't think that he really meant what he said about being "just a man." I thought he was just talking and expressing his inner thoughts—which he often did.

I didn't really take it to heart, and didn't really believe him. He was always saying something in his sermons to see how we would react—sometimes it was better not to react, and to take it all in. I still thought he was God. To me, he was the most incredible man on the planet—and I would have done (almost) anything for him.

One time, when he was in Hilo, I overheard Yahowah say, "I think it is time we disperse The Family. Everyone takes their children and goes their separate ways." Things were so calm there, I think he wanted more action, adventure, and excitement.

After a few weeks in Hilo, Yahowah decided to go to Oahu to watch Mercury break the world record of hang gliding off Makapu'u cliffs. Yahowah left for Oahu with a few women and men, while most of the rest of us stayed behind in Hilo. At the time, I didn't think anything of it.

When Yahowah and his entourage went to Lanikai, they decided to stay in Jupiter's place—a round glass house which sat up on a hill overlooking the ocean above Lanikai beach. Even though Yahowah was in Lanikai, we in Hilo still had morning meditations in the ballroom of the Doc Hill Mansion, and listened to tapes and chanted. We always stayed completely connected to him.

As usual, Monday morning, August 25, we had our morning meditation listening to tapes of Yahowah and chanting. After class, we all sat around. Some went to work and to perform duties, and others were together talking and starting their day.

Then the pay phone outside the Doc Hill mansion started to ring. This was strange because the phone never rang before. Sunflower went outside to answer it. I was with Jupiter sitting in meditation class after it was over, hanging out and talking.

Suddenly Sunflower ran into the ballroom and said that Father was in a hang gliding accident. I was so confused as to why Yahowah would go hang gliding. Jupiter was furious because he knew that Father had never been on a hang glider. Jupiter was an expert hang glider himself, and knew how dangerous this sport was. The next thing I knew, Jupiter jumped up and said, "What the fuck did he do? Who does he think he is?" Jupiter said that he had to get to Lanikai right away and check out what happened.

We all became increasingly worried that something terrible came down. We also had little communication with the Council Women who were there with him. Only that one phone call.

I thought that Yahowah had to be okay—I only thought the best of outcomes.

We all walked around in a daze that morning until the afternoon, feeling concerned. Then, around 5:30 p.m. we received another phone call from one of the women in Lanikai. This time she said that Yahowah passed away. He left the body at 5:20 p.m.—nine hours after the accident.

Everyone went into shock. I couldn't believe he died from this. As I started to realize that it had really happened, I never cried so hard in my life. The pain in my heart was like a knife stabbing me. What would this mean? How could the women let him do this? All throughout the house, it sounded like crying babies—both the women and men. For a core group of us—those who were there for the love of Father—it was especially painful. The children were so confused and didn't understand what was happening.

The day that we found out Yahowah passed away, there was a lot of anger (and negativity) amongst the Family members. Which was unusual. Because we didn't thoroughly understand what happened—and we didn't understand the reality of it. And we had no details. We had to make it up in our minds. We were all wondering: "*What the F—were they thinking?!*" But then we realized that it was all Yahowah's choice. And once he made up his mind—that's it. There was nothing anyone could do or say to change it.

Yahowah's Final Hours

A couple of days later, we received tapes in Hilo with recordings of what had happened on that fateful day. Isis recorded everything in The Family, including Father's pain while he was passing away. We all gathered into the meditation room and began to play the tapes. As we listened in awe and grief, we heard as the events unfolded.

Early that day, during morning meditation in Lanikai, Yahowah began talking about the old Lemuria—a "lost continent" that sank into the ocean, which was the homeland of human ancestors. Yahowah said: "This was the home of the Gods when man first came to earth . . . he came half in the body of a bird and half in the body of a man. This is according to the evolutionary plan . . . Ancient Lemurian men used to climb to the top of these peaks and go off . . ."

Yahowah believed that he could access his memories from a Lemurian past life, and therefore would know how to fly. Yahowah turned to Mercury and said, "So let's go flying, Mercury. You got a kite big enough for me? . . . I would like to be up there before or around the time the sun is coming up . . . It is all in the evolutionary plan, so let's go Mercury . . . Let me jump off the top of a mountain again."

The women gathered around Yahowah pleading for him not to go. What kind of person jumps off a cliff, with no hang gliding lessons? But there was no stopping Yahowah. He was determined to do what he was going to do.

In the car ride on the way to Makapu'u cliffs, Yahowah said, "Jumping off the top of the mountain will prove my thesis. The memory is deep in my subconscious. I will call upon it and I will know exactly what to do in any given situation . . . Everything must be tested by life experience . . . You have to tap into that subconscious . . . Besides that, Makushla, Jesus is in the air, so what could happen to me? Jesus would not let any hurt come to his own Father, so I'm OK. Don't worry, I will be fine."

As we listened to the tapes playing, we could all feel the ominous foreboding in Yahowah's words. We knew where this day was leading to, and it was absolutely crushing to hear Yahowah and those around him as he marched toward his final earthly moments.

Yahowah reassured everyone: "I would never commit suicide. I fully expect to be successful, I have no doubt in my mind. I don't know how I am going to land without a scratch, there is always someplace. And I know one thing, I am going to come down this day and live to tell it . . . unless, of course, my Father sees differently. That must always be taken into consideration. His will be done. Not my will. He may see it—far out—this is the perfect time for Yahowah to leave and in the perfect way."

He continued, "Can you imagine the headlines? Can you imagine the curiosity, a 53 year old man? (laughing) Ha, Ha, Ha, Ha—if anything, they would want to know more about this character. I have no plans or thoughts on the matter. (singing) Life suddenly looks so good. Look at the sunlight "

As I heard these words, I thought back to what Yahowah had said just a week earlier when he was in Hilo—how he was considering dispersing The Family, and how he seemed to be getting bored and ready to move on. Was he actually suicidal? Did he plan to jump off that cliff on purpose to end his earthly journey?

As Yahowah and the entourage made their way up Makapu'u Cliffs, they encountered a locked gate, preventing their access to the top. The gate contained 12 locks, and a broken 13th lock lay on the ground. Yahowah was intent on moving ahead, and asked if someone there could break the 12 locks with a rock. No one volunteered.

Just then, another hang glider appeared, who Father had met before and named The Black Knight. He saw them and unlocked the gate so they could proceed. Yahowah took this as a fortuitous sign, saying, "See! An angel has arrived. It is meant to be." They continued to the top of the cliff, nearly 1000 feet above the ocean.

We could hear on the tapes as it sounded like the women tried to stop him, but to no avail. Once Yahowah made up his mind to do something, it was next to impossible to change it. Still, we were all furious with them, and with Mercury—and The Black Knight. That gate was locked for a reason—not to let just anyone fly off Makapu'u. It was no place for beginners.

At the top of the ridge, Mercury helped Yahowah onto the hang glider. This was the point of no return. Yahowah turned to Mercury and said, "Okay, son, check it out." And with that, he leapt off the cliff. At that very moment, the wind suddenly stopped and Yahowah plunged down hundreds of feet. All the women screamed in horror.

As he neared the ground, somehow Yahowah gained some control of the hang glider and curved upwards and out toward the ocean. Amazing. Maybe he would be OK after all. He circled over the ocean for several minutes, and then everyone watched as he returned towards the shore and crashed into the beach, landing hard on his backside, laying motionless.

From their vantage on the top of the cliffs, the women were unsure exactly what happened. Makushla gushed, "It was the perfect landing! I bet he does not have a scratch or a dirty spot on him. He has done it—he has mastered everything." Isis added, "Miracles everywhere! We have two bottles of champagne at home." Heaven shouted, "Victory!"

Listening to their optimistic assessments, I felt a pit in my stomach.

Everyone then made their way down the mountain to find Father on the beach, where he was surrounded by curious locals. Police, a fire truck, and an ambulance were already on the scene. Yahowah was dazed but alive, and he began chatting in Samoan with a local guy. As the women approached him, Yahowah said, "Where did that angel go that led me down? What's happening?"

Someone there suggested that they let the paramedics take Yahowah to the hospital. Makusha disagreed, saying, "No, he's fine. He is just in the bliss—he is just enjoying the bliss. Look at his face—he is in the bliss."

Amazingly, Yahowah was smiling and laughing as he said, "I thought that I was going to fly the kite. I guess it was God's last lesson he had to teach me."

The women and Mercury took Yahowah into their Mercedes and they made their way back home. Yahowah slowly began regaining his consciousness, and with that came waves of pain. Yahowah told them, "My back is broken at the base."

Back in the Lanikai house, they brought Yahowah into the living room and laid him out on the floor. We all winced as we heard him crying out in pain. Despite his anguish, he was assuring everyone, "Well this I know just as surely as I am laying here . . . that it is all positive. Such an energy in my lower back, it is incredible. I am comfortable, sweethearts. Best made plans of mice and men oft go astray."

The women tried to ease his pain, propping him up with pillows and offering him sacred herb and champagne. But it sounded like his pain only seemed to get worse, as he howled and released pressure, saying, "The opposite of this must be bliss. For all polarities prevail."

As I was listening to the tapes, I could hear that Yahowah was in pain. I felt that someone needed to make decisions on Yahowah's behalf. I noticed the women trying to figure out what to do. But it didn't sound like there was one clear path to get help.

At one point Yahowah suggested, "Maybe I should go to the hospital." Makushla dismissed the idea, saying, "We can get a chiropractor to come here, you should stay here. We can get you some painkillers." Yahowah acquiesced, saying, "Alright, get me some painkillers. I think I am in the hands of God. Oh, God take me—really I have learned all my lessons."

Then he was hit with another wave of shooting pains, and through his cries he again said, "Ah let me go to the hospital." Makushla replied, "Oh, Yahowah, please it doesn't feel right to have you go to the hospital." Yahowah agreed, saying, "Alright. I won't go to the hospital."

Yahowah began crying and screaming in pain, echoed by women crying in the background. He must have known how bad this was. Mercury brought Yahowah some sacred snow (cocaine) and Heaven said, "Yahowah, cocaine won't relieve the pain. I know it. Anyway, let him have it—it wouldn't hurt." And Yahowah took it.

An Adept (as we referred to the chiropractor) arrived at the house and attended to Yahowah, asking those assembled, "Who is he?" Makushla and the women responded, "He is God." As Yahowah released pressure and cried out in agony, he said, "I am not God. Man, he is God. I am nothing. Man is everything. Oh God, help me. Oh God, end it."

Yahowah asked the women to call Yogi Bhajan, and he spoke with him on the phone. Yogi reassured Yahowah, saying, "God bless you, you take care. I love you. Everything will be okay. Sat Nam, God Bless." Yahowah replied, "Love you, son."

While we were listening, we mostly heard Yahowah moaning and groaning in pain. It was difficult for us to understand that they didn't accept medical help. It sounded like they decided to let him ride it out . . . and never thought that the outcome would be his final day. This is one example of not thinking for yourself. And the ultimate happened. He passed away.

I don't think that it was planned. And I think they were following Yahowah's teachings. I'm not sure what I would have done in that situation. I may have done the same thing. We were all taught that you don't go to the hospital unless you break a bone. Of course—how would they have known if he broke a bone, or not, if he didn't go to the hospital? Why they didn't go is a mystery to me.

It was clear to me that Yahowah was in agony and needed medical attention. He needed help, other than chanting and praying and reassuring him that it was going to all be okay. On the other hand, it was his choice. And we were following him. When Yahowah was hurt—the problem is that *no one could think for themselves.*

I wasn't there. But maybe if I was, I would have fallen apart and not been able to handle it. There was a lot of strength and composure from the women who experienced it. They seemed so sure that they were doing the right thing. It was mind-blowing to me. Maybe that is why he chose those 12 Council Women, because of their strength.

Life's River

Once we found out he passed away, we all got into the chanting for three days—non-stop around the clock. It was Yahowah's teachings that once a person passes away, their soul needs to review their Life's River for three and a half days. This way they can take the lessons learned and move onto the next life. Once they review the lessons that they have learned, then they can come back to the Earth evolved, and not take that same Karma with them. For that reason, they didn't want to cremate or bury the body before three and a half days, so that this could happen.

For three days, the women cleaned him and bathed him, candles burning, always two people there chanting and watching over his body. During that time, his body started to decompose. They called the coroners after three and half days to pick him up.

While all of this was going on, back in Hilo we still had children to take care of. We weren't allowed to tell anybody about what happened to Yahowah—it had to be a secret. We purposely didn't tell anybody what had happened, because we didn't want the authorities to come and take his body away. When the coroner later conducted an autopsy, it came back that Yahowah had broken his sternum. So I guess he did break a bone, but it wasn't something visible to the eye.

Once everybody found out what happened, it became a huge newsworthy story in Lanikai, Hawaii, and beyond. The phone was ringing off the hook. Everybody was coming by. Members who had left The Family returned and were paying their respects. The after-effects became somewhat chaotic as we were all grieving.

We had to figure out how to continue on with running The Family. It was so hard to believe that this was true. This was not an ending that any of us could prepare for. We were supposed to be the survivors. It was a shock. And no one knew what would happen next. We had lost our leader, Our Father. Our God.

The Visit

A few days after Yahowah died, his former wife and children—Elaine Baker, Ben, and Bart—came to Hawaii to check on their Dad. Elaine and Jim's other son, Beau, was unable to attend that trip. When they arrived, that's when they found out that Yahowah had passed away. No one had called them to alert them of their Father's passing. They found out from a former member, Atla, who had heard about the accident and death.

I had to get my act together and be a hostess. Everybody was in a state of grief, and so no one wanted to entertain them—because they were Yahowah's Piscean children. So everyone made me hang out with them all day long. That was very difficult for me, because I was really grieving. And I didn't know what to say to Bart, knowing how horrible it must have been for him.

Bart wanted to talk to me and came to see us at the Doc Hill

Mansion. I was still with Starman at this point, but of course I came down to talk with him. We were standing a distance apart from one another. Bart was so upset and wanted to know what happened, from my point of view.

Bart and I used to be together, but now he barely recognized me. I was no longer the Laurel Canyon girl. After many months in the islands, I had golden dark skin, long golden brown hair, and a baby.

I walked out and greeted him on the grass area by the oceanside. I was devastated and sad. Not sure what to even say to his son. When I first saw him, I went up to him and touched his shoulder. He was somewhat approachable, but not his warm and friendly self.

I said, "I am so sad and sorry for your loss."

He started talking about the pain in his heart. He just could not comprehend why his father went hang gliding. I was quiet and listened. And I couldn't even respond to what he said. We both looked out at the ocean and started crying. This would be the last time that I would see Bart in The Source Family.

I explained to Bart what was happening and told him everything that I knew. At that point, I knew very little about what had happened. All that I knew was that Yahowah went hang gliding, lost control of the kite, got caught in a turbulent wind, barreled down, and landed in a tree on Makapu'u Beach. I was also mad and angry and confused.

Bart told me that the day the hang gliding incident happened, "Atla"—a former Family member—had called and told him that she had heard that something had happened to Yahowah and that he might want to check into it. Bart then phoned the Glass

House, and Isis answered. Bart told her that he wanted to talk to his Dad.

Isis told Bart, "Your father doesn't want to talk to you."

There are two ways to look at the situation: (1) Isis was following Father's orders; or (2) Isis should have thought for herself and done what was right. What Isis could have said was: "Your father was in a hang gliding accident and can't talk to you right now." Why couldn't Isis tell Bart the truth? That Father was on the ground in excruciating pain, and maybe not in a position to talk to his son. Of course, Bart wouldn't have known that or understood that at the time.

Hearing these words, Bart was absolutely devastated. He flashed back to two years earlier, when he had called The Father House, and Isis told Bart, "Your dad doesn't want to talk to you anymore . . . until you join The Family." According to Bart, it was at this moment that his father had "died" in his eyes. And he never talked to his dad again.

Yahowah

Chapter 10

THE COUNTRY CLUB

The Other Woman

September 1975

After Yahowah left his body, the whole Family dynamic changed. It was just natural for the Council Women and Makushla to take over the Family decisions. Nobody was prepared for this to happen. So they just winged it.

I know Yahowah's women were in complete shock. They lost their love, husband, and Father. Now they had all these decisions to make for all 144 of us. Yahowah did not give the responsibility to anyone specific. I just assumed that they would keep The Family going, just like Yahowah did. But that's not what happened.

For the first few weeks, the Family members and I felt so lost and confused. When we were at the Hilo House, after Yahowah passed, Sunflower became the head of The Family—*in my eyes*. He was the first member of The Family (#1 on the list).

Once the Council Women left Oahu and came back to Hilo to join the rest of us, Makushla became the head of The Family and the Council Women. It seemed like she would be the likely person to continue on with his teachings. My impression was that Makushla didn't feel comfortable being the leader of our Family (she was still in her early 20s). She often would ask other Family members to lead morning meditations.

Aura (Starman's second woman) had her baby around September 16, 1975. I was at her birth in Hilo, at the Governor's House (aka The Doc Hill Mansion) on the beach. Aura had a horrible delivery. The baby came out feet first in a breech position. In order to deliver the baby, who came fast and furious—because it was too late to do anything else—Soma (the midwife) reacted quickly and tried to turn the baby around. As I watched in horror, she wasn't able to turn around the baby. So she decided to deliver the baby feet first.

Soma grabbed the feet and pulled the baby out with the help of Aura pushing. It looked like Soma had done this before—but I had never seen this done with any of the other deliveries. I was too young to comment and say anything, so I just watched.

The baby was a girl and she was named Grace. She was small but adorable with big blue eyes. After she was born, everything seemed to go well and mother and baby were settling in nicely. A few days later, Aura got really sick with fever and chills—she was going delirious. Her condition accelerated fast and Starman wasn't sure what to do.

Yahowah always said that we don't go to the hospital unless it's for a broken bone. So we all tried to figure out how to help Aura. Yahowah had passed away and it was now up to us to make leadership decisions. This was new territory for all of us. We had to think for ourselves.

Starman wasn't able to make a decision—he was freaking out

and hysterical. Sunflower suggested, "We have to take her to the hospital. Or she's going to die." He took it upon himself to call 911. In my opinion, Sunflower saved her life.

The ambulance took Aura to a little cottage hospital in Hilo. Right away, Starman called Aura's mom, who flew over and took over all medical decisions. The first night that Aura was in the hospital, she almost died. It turns out that Aura had a staph infection throughout her body.

While Aura was receiving medical care, all of the nursing moms chipped in and took turns taking care of her baby, Grace. I stayed home and took care of Grace while Starman went to the hospital daily.

Meanwhile, staph took over the whole inside of Aura's body. Aura could have died if she didn't get the proper care. Thank God Sunflower acted so fast to have her taken into the local hospital. And also . . . that he could think for himself.

When Aura's mom arrived in Hilo at the Hospital, I was there with Starman. And, if looks could kill. She looked at me like I was the most evil person on the planet. I really don't blame her that much. She probably thought we were all nuts.

The Hilo hospital wanted to move Aura to Oahu—to Queen's Hospital. Aura's mom paid for Starman, Stardust, Grace and me to fly to Oahu and she rented us a little house in Kailua to stay in. This way we could be close to Aura.

This was a very difficult time for our little family. I wasn't sure how the outcome would be. Aura was so sick and fragile. I felt horrible for Aura. When she came out of the hospital, she was so weak and thin. It took her months to get her strength and get back to good health—and the entire time, she couldn't nurse her baby.

For most of the babies in The Family—you would nurse for three years. I nursed Stardust until she was three years old. Not all the time, but it was available to her as needed. This was common practice in The Family. Yahowah always preached that all the babies are to be nursed for three years. My mom never nursed me and my sisters, when we were babies. In that generation, they didn't nurse as much.

Once Aura was feeling better, her mom flew back to Los Angeles, and Aura, Starman, Stardust, Grace and I moved back to Hilo to rejoin the rest of The Family.

Hills of Hilo

While Aura was recovering in the hospital, the whole Family left the Doc Hill Mansion and moved into The Country Club up in the hills above Hilo. This was, at one time, a Golf Country Club—since abandoned. At the time, I didn't know the reason why we had to move from the Doc Hill Mansion to the Hilo Country Club—I later found out that it was sold to a family, so we had to move.

The Country Club was three stories and had a guesthouse, and lots of land. Plenty of places to hang out and relax. Lots of rolling hills with grass for the babies to play. It was like country life on The Big Island—less like a beach community and more like mountain life.

The main house was spacious and had lots of room to move around in. The bathrooms and showers were downstairs. The top floor had a huge ballroom where we held morning meditation. It was plenty big for all of us to sleep comfortably. Most of the nursing mothers and babies slept on the porch with a screen around the patio. There were beds lined up along the porch. We slept comfortably as the weather in Hilo was cooler than most of the island.

Secret Trip to the Health Food Store

After Yahowah died, money got tight and our basic necessities were not always met. We were all trying to figure out how to run The Family, like we used to. But it just wasn't the same. There was a shortage of food and I was always hungry. I mostly ate brown rice, avocados, papayas, mangos, bananas, and some vegetables. I got used to eating very little. I was still nursing Stardust and it felt like I wasn't getting enough nutrition. She took everything from me.

We were so desperate for calories, and had so much time on our hands, that we resorted to foraging for food. Sometimes a few nursing mothers and I would go down the street and find a macadamia nut tree. I would shake the tree for nuts to fall down. Then we would sit at the side of the road and crack one nut at a time with a big rock. Sometimes we would be there for hours filling our bellies up with macadamia nuts. We would always talk about: "If we could eat anything, what would it be?" I wished for cheese, eggs, and milk. Those were my dream foods. Also chocolate would be a sin for me.

The men were fishing for ahi tuna, which became one of our staple foods. The men would bring home the fish—which were huge—and cut them open on the kitchen counter to clean them. As they cut open the fish, inside were tons of other sea creatures. It was disgusting to watch, but we were hungry, and we ate it.

However, from the fish (we speculated)—some of the Family members contracted hepatitis and started turning yellow—including the whites of their eyes. And their pee was brown like Coca-Cola. This was a major event. We all got it at the same time. Fortunately, the kids didn't get it.

We were wiped out. It sucked all the energy out of you. So exhausted. I could barely move—lying down on the floor with the other nursing mothers. To cure ourselves, we all went on a carrot juice fast. It would take weeks and weeks for us all to slowly recover.

In the midst of our hunger and disease—one day Anastasia received some money from her mom. She said, "Let's drive down to the Hilo Health Food Store and buy whatever we want." This sounded like a great idea. Anastasia, Azure and I devised a plan: to "borrow" one of the blue vans and drive down to Hilo with the babies—and not tell anyone. I was very nervous about this, but totally on board with the adventure.

First we had to figure out which van to steal and then find the car keys. It was decided that Anastasia would drive the van—I didn't have a driver's license, nor could I drive. We found the keys, and when no one was around, we all three and our babies snuck out into the van and covertly drove away. It felt like we were doing something so bad and I was so scared of getting into trouble with the Council Women.

As Anastasia backed out of the driveway, Azure and I and the babies ducked down to hide. All the while praying to God that we make it. We were so hungry and couldn't wait to eat some goodies, cheese, or dates.

On our exhilarating drive down the mountain we all laughed

hysterically. The babies were so good and quiet. We finally made it to the Health Food Store, parked the car and walked in. We each picked out the foods that we craved. It was the most excited that I had felt in a long time.

As we were in the back of the store, I heard a familiar voice at the cash register. To my horror, it was Harvest Moon, Makushla, and Astral buying cheese, eggs, and dates for the Council Women. I quickly ran to the back of the store to tell Anastasia and Azure that they were here.

We couldn't believe that—all this time—the Council Women were eating differently than we did. Here we were starving, and all the time they were eating dairy foods. This is the way the Council Women decided to lead our Family. It felt contradictory to what Father believed he wanted The Family to be—a family that shared equally everything from food to essential needs. This changed when Father passed away. I believe this is one reason why The Family didn't survive longevity.

We all freaked out and hid in the back with the babies and our food. My heart was pumping out of my body. Luckily the babies didn't make a sound. We waited for the Council Women to leave so we could run out of the store. We all knew that if they found us buying food (and stealing the van) we would be in deep trouble. I'm not exactly sure what they would do to us. Would they kick us out of The Family? Anything was possible and unpredictable. Not to mention, we weren't allowed to eat those foods.

After they left we busted up laughing and decided to stay and buy our goodies. We paid for our items and then walked across the street to the park and had a picnic. We couldn't stop laughing and being grateful that we (barely) pulled it off. After our lavish picnic it was time to head back before the men started to arrive home from work. Once again we drove off, back up the mountain, scared that someone would recognize us. Thanks be to God, we made it back unscathed. This became our little secret for the rest of The Family days.

State of Shock

November 29, 1975

It was a typical early morning meditation. I had set up Starman's mat and got his coffee. I decided to go to the restroom before class. It was 4:15 a.m. and I had fifteen minutes before 4:30 a.m. meditation class. Stardust was sleeping on the patio with all the other babies and a few moms to watch over them. I went downstairs to the bottom level where all the bathrooms were. Now it was 4:28 a.m.—and as I was walking out the door, the earth started to shake violently. I knew this was an earthquake and ran out to the lawn area away from the house.

As I watched, the huge house tilted off its foundation, one side at a time. In the distance, I could see smoke and lava spewing out of the volcano, and then lightning. The next thing I knew, everyone was running out of the house like a stampede. I was in shock and froze. The earth wouldn't stop shaking and we all lost our balance.

I knew Stardust was in danger—upstairs by herself. But I couldn't go and get her. Too many people running down the stairs. Unbeknownst to me, Ocean (one of my good friends, a brother in

The Family) grabbed Stardust with her blanket and brought her to me. Ocean wrapped her up to cover her face and ran outside to meet me. He and Stardust were the last people to exit the house.

Then, all of a sudden, we could hear the windows shattering and breaking right where the babies were sleeping. Ocean really was my hero and thought fast to pick her up. Stardust was sound asleep and didn't even wake up. Meanwhile the earthquake kept going and the volcano kept erupting. It was so dark and you could see the lava coming out of the volcano, even though it was far away. We all gathered on the lawn and huddled, far enough away from the house. I could hear glass breaking and loud noises coming out of the house.

No one wanted to go back into the house for weeks. We all slept outside, except for a few brave souls. For a couple of days we stayed at the property. Finally, some of the men drove to Hilo downtown to check it out. That's when we learned that a tsunami wave hit Black Sands Beach and killed many Boy Scouts and their leaders in the early morning hours. That the earthquake was 8.0 off the coast of Hilo. It was later downsized to 7.5. Hilo and the Big Island were devastated.

Shortly after the earthquake, I knew that I wanted off this island. I think everyone felt the same way. The ground shook for many months with aftershocks. I had never experienced an earthquake as violent as this one. Los Angeles had many earthquakes, but this was different. Being on an island in the middle of the ocean somehow seemed worse. Was our world coming to an end?

The Family in Lanikai greeting the sun

Chapter 11

PARADISE FOUND

Becoming Heartstar

Winter-Spring 1976

When Yahowah died it opened up a new path for me. I started to think for myself. I had to figure it out as I went along. I stayed with Starman and Aura—I was stuck, but loyal and committed. He was the father of Stardust and I couldn't imagine the thought of actually leaving him—even though it had been on my mind for a while. I just didn't know how, or have any support to make such a bold move.

In February 1976 we all moved from the Big Island to Lanikai Beach on the island of Oahu. In Lanikai we had three to four houses for all of us to live in. The house I lived in was called Paradise Found. (We always named our houses.) It was on the beach and all the mothers and children were put in this house—which was good for me to hang out with all of them. We all still got up at 4:00 a.m., did our exercises, jumped into the ocean in the dark under the stars, and then showered and went to morning meditation at The Sun Palace down the street—where The Council Women and all of Yahowah's children lived.

Morning meditation was different now. Makushla was forced to lead it. I don't think she was comfortable doing this. The Council Women seemed to make all the important decisions now. The Family tried so hard to stay together and follow Yahowah teachings. But it just didn't cut it for most of us.

One day at class Makushla asked for me to bring Stardust to her. Stardust sat on Makushla's lap, and Makushla was petting her gently admiring her beauty. Suddenly Makushla looked at me, then looked at Stardust, and back at me and said, "Your new name is Heartstar. This is a more fitting name for you."

I didn't question it. My new name made sense to me because I was a mother to Stardust and a woman to Starman and my best friend was Belle Star. I was so happy to no longer be a vegetable (Mushroom). Only the members that stayed during this time knew about my new name. I felt like I was becoming Heartstar—age 18 and growing up.

Later Makushla told me that she was the person who had mostly named everyone in The Family. It was very common to have your name changed—at different times—in the commune, and it really did have a profound effect on who you became and how others related to you. Right away, I adjusted to my new name. As Heartstar, I felt like I changed dramatically. I felt stronger and started to have a voice and think for myself.

Should I Stay Or Should I Go

Around that time, I felt strong enough to let Starman know how I felt—and that I wanted to leave him, and take Stardust with me. I wanted his blessings, and hoped that he would be okay with it—and that we could remain close friends—for Stardust's sake.

His reaction was mostly emotionless—it was not what I expected, and he had very little to say. He told me that he didn't want me to leave, and basically said that I could not go—but he said this without conviction. It sounded like he was just saying it to say it—but that he didn't really mean it.

I realized that I had stayed all that time to not confront him about me leaving, and it turned out that it was no big deal at all. I couldn't believe it.

Soon it became well known that Starman and I were no longer in a relationship, even though I stayed in the house with him for Stardust's sake. She adored him and I didn't have the heart to seperate them. My mind was going a mile a minute with how this was going to work. I just prayed and believed that something would come to me.

Things were getting more and more strange for Starman and me. We didn't talk much or spend time together. He seemed more interested in Aura, and I grew further away from him. This made it a little easier for me to want to leave. I stayed with him solely because he was Stardust's father—but this could only carry me so far.

I was starting to grow up and recognize this relationship was not a long-term one—and the inevitable was going to happen. It was still extremely hard for me to convince myself this wasn't working out. We had been so happy before—why not be happy now? It was clear that it was over. Starman knew it. So did I.

Moving On

Everyday I swam in the ocean to the little island off the Lanikai coast with Stardust on my back. This was how my days became full. Of course I hung out with my favorite sisters on the beach. Sometimes I would hitch a ride on catamarans sailing by. Most of the time I was playing in the water and swimming with Stardust.

I became really anxious to move on and was looking for an exit strategy. Several of the men were interested in me, but I wasn't interested in them. The only person I liked was Sir Knight. He wasn't in Lanikai very much, but we seemed closer than friends and I thought it was possible he felt the same way about me.

I thought he had a thing for me. He was always flirting with me—more like a friendship, or so I thought. He knew that I was unattached to Starman and that I wanted to leave him. The last time that Sir Knight came to Lanikai, he said, "You can come and stay with me anytime you want." I was so grateful for Sir Knight and hoped that it would work out to be with him someday.

I really admired Sir Knight for all the ways he helped us nursing mothers. Sir Knight was mostly working on the Farm on the Big Island in a secluded spot. He was growing the sacred herb with an investor and selling it to make money for The Family to survive. At this point, the money he made from selling the sacred herb comprised the majority of the Family's finances. When he came to visit us in Lanikai, he would often go to the market with his extra money and buy the mothers cheese, dates, eggs, bread, and sometimes chocolate.

We ended up having a long, flirtatious relationship. "Long"

means a few months—this was considered a long time in The Family. Sir Knight had a charming English accent, big blue eyes, and blonde hair. He was kind and ambitious and I trusted him with me and Stardust. I was contemplating that he may be someone who I could have a relationship with.

I knew that Sir Knight was on a farm and making money to help The Family survive, but I didn't know quite where that farm was. It didn't even matter to me where it was. All I knew was that I wanted to be with Sir Knight. And that I wanted to be rescued and taken to his farm.

One day, Sir Knight was leaving to go back to the farm on the Big Island. Something came over me that I had no control over. Before he left, I gave him a big kiss, deep with passion. I was hoping that this kiss would symbolize that I wanted to be his woman. I think he got the message that I was interested in him. Soon after he left, I wrote Sir Knight many letters saying how I felt about him. This was the only form of communication we had. We exchanged love letters back and forth.

When I found out that he would be coming back to Lanikai soon, I decided to call the farm to ask Sir Knight if I could return with him back to the farm for a while. I spoke on the phone with One (a Family member—yes, that was his name), and One promised to relay the message to him. One ran out to the bay, where Sir Knight was swimming with dolphins, and shouted, "Sir Knight, Heartstar called!"

I sat by the landline phone at the Paradise Found house and waited—and soon enough it rang. It was Sir Knight, and I was elated when he said that he was excited for me to come join him, and he was so supportive. I was so happy that he was receptive to me going with him. He said he would pay for Stardust and me to fly over to the Big Island.

Escape With Sir Knight

Since Starman didn't want me to leave, I hatched a plan for me and Stardust to secretly escape in the middle of the night, while Starman and everyone else was sleeping. I had voiced to Sir Knight that I was afraid of Starman's reaction to me leaving. The only thing is that I couldn't tell anyone—we thought it would be best if our plan was kept under wraps, imagining that there might be some resistance.

I knew that Starman, Makushla, and the Council Women would not be okay with me leaving, but I was tired of starving and staying with someone who I didn't love and who didn't care if I stayed or not. Even though I was scared to do this, I really wanted to get out. Once again, a moment of truth—I made an important decision that would change my life forever.

Sir Knight got word to me via a letter that he was buying me a ticket to fly over to Kona. He wanted me to pack what I could and tell no one that I was leaving and going to stay with him on the farm. He suggested I take a taxi to Honolulu airport to keep the secret. I was so excited to leave and escape the Lanikai commune and move on to the next chapter.

I was sad, in a way, to take Stardust away from her father. I hoped he would understand and always be in her life. I knew he had Aura as his woman and Grace, their baby. I also thought that he was over being with me and didn't really care that I left.

The next letter from Sir Knight had a ticket for Stardust and me and some money for a taxi. This became so real that I was now leaving for good—or was it just temporary? I had no idea how this relationship would turn out.

Finally the day came. I waited until it was late at night and everyone was sound asleep. I never went to sleep that night and waited for the time to sneak out. The taxi drove up to Paradise Found, and I bundled up Stardust in her favorite blanket. I grabbed a few things and quietly went outside to the taxi—the only car on the street. Stardust was still sleeping and it was windy outside and dark. The sky was full of stars and the ocean was swishing in the distance.

Stardust and I made it to the airport late at night. My heart was pounding that I had escaped. At least that's what it felt like. Really, anytime if someone wanted to leave The Family, they could. We got on the plane and flew over to Kona. I couldn't wait to see Sir Knight and start our adventure together. I knew this wasn't going to go over well with the Council Women. But I didn't care anymore.

We arrived in Kona—and there he was, with his piercing blue eyes shining against the moonlit sky and a smile from ear to ear. Sir Knight greeted me with open arms and a big kiss, and his embrace assured me that we were doing the right thing. I didn't even look back and prayed that no one saw me leave. I felt so bad that I was doing this. It was one of the scariest things I had ever done. My mind was buzzing with all these thoughts of the unknown and I looked forward to seeing how this would work out.

I think Sir Knight was blown away that I actually left Starman. I was one of the most devoted members in The Family and one of the first to join. But my main reason for being in The Family was Yahowah, and now that he had left his earthly body and was gone, I was changing rapidly and wanted a new start.

Honomalino Bay

After arriving in Kona, we drove in Sir Knight's 1976 Toyota Scout to a small harbor named Miloli'i Fishing Village. That's where his little boat was ready to take us to Honomalino Bay. We shopped at the local market for food and essentials, loaded the boat, and sailed off to the farm.

His boat was small and only had two benches to sit on. It was a beautiful ride, even though the ocean was choppy, with the wind picking up. Stardust was so cute and was up to the adventure. She was just over a year old and didn't understand what was going on. The house was about one mile away from the village and it took about thirty minutes to get there. I don't remember seeing anyone else sail by. By this time of day, it was hot and humid—but the wind blowing the ocean water onto our faces cooled us down.

We finally arrived at Honomalino Bay. It was a small bay and you could see the house in the distance amongst the tropical trees. We docked the boat and took Stardust out. Then Sir Knight walked us up to the house. It was a two story house with an open plan. Outside in the back, there was a makeshift kitchen, a fire pit, and a water tank. Lots of tropical plants virtually covered the house. It was very secluded and private, however there was electricity and phone lines.

Sir Knight lived in this house—along with his investor

partner on the project, who was there some of the time—which was located not too far away from the pot farm. Now Stardust and I would live there too. Sir Knight loved Stardust and was so good with her. We spent many days swimming in the ocean and taking long walks with Stardust. At night we would sit by a bonfire and sing or chant. It was so calm and quiet not having so many people around all the time. It gave me a chance to reflect on my life and future.

Sir Knight went to unload the groceries and the few things that I brought. We set up our stuff in the house—and our adventure began. Sir Knight and I had a love affair. We spent a lot of time together alone at first. Once we put Stardust to sleep, we had the whole place to ourselves. After many months of being in an estranged relationship with Starman, it was pure pleasure being with Sir Knight and experiencing a physical and emotional love. We would swim naked and free under the stars and the moon, free from having hundreds of other Family members around. It was intimate and exciting and I experienced love in a more sensual way. It was less of a spiritual intimacy and became more of physical lust.

I didn't know much about the pot farm and I didn't ask him about it. All I knew was this was a source of income for The Family and his investor was looking to make some money to pay back his boss. Sir Knight was so excited and proud to show me the farm and his crops. The plants were big and there were plenty of them. Other workers were also there and some of The Family brothers came over from Lanikai to help.

On one of our adventures we decided to go into the village for groceries and dinner. By the time we were finished, it was dark and getting stormy—in Hawaii the weather could change rapidly. The only way back to the house was by boat—we got into the boat in a storm. Imagine torrential rain, huge 10-15 foot waves, and the wind hitting this tiny little boat. Stardust and I hung on to each other for dear life—but she thought it was like a roller coaster and was laughing. Meanwhile I thought we were going to die.

Sir Knight was visibly concerned as he struggled to maintain control of the little boat from flipping over. I trusted Sir Knight to get us back. He navigated the motorboat as best as he could as waves were crashing over us and the wind was howling. The boat was rocking fiercely and water was pouring into our little boat. It took us double the time to get back—as we were going against the current.

Once we made it to the bay, I jumped out of the boat with Stardust and kissed the ground. I think Sir Knight was exhausted from the experience. I know I was exhausted. I have no idea what we were thinking about taking this little boat back in the middle of those bad weather conditions.

About a month after my arrival at the farm, Prism (one of the main Council Women—and mother of one of Yahowah's babies, Buttercup) decided to come over from Lanikai to hang out with Sir Knight. And to her surprise I was there already cohabitating with him. Apparently (and unbeknownst to me) she had a crush on Sir Knight. It seemed strange that she would just show up out of the blue—I don't think that Sir Knight was happy that she had showed up unannounced—but it was next to impossible to say no to one of the Council Women. I'm guessing that she told the Council Women that I was there.

Once again, I was in a relationship with a second woman. It was fine with me to share him, because I adored Prism. Prism kept Sir Knight very busy with Dhyanism. I was left with not being attached to a man. I needed to not have an ego about their relationship. I found out later that the Council Women and Makushla didn't want her to be there—and were furious with her for going and leaving Lanikai.

The Crop Harvest

The marijuana crop was growing rapidly. I would walk over to the farm with Sir Knight occasionally to check on the growth. There were hundreds of plants sprawling and blending in with the Hawaiian plants. I could smell the aroma of the sacred herb as I walked closer. The plants were as tall as me, and beautiful to behold.

Sir Knight would tell me how much money these plants would generate for The Family. He was so thrilled to be a part of such a great source of income for us and his investors. This crop was so well planned out and calculated financially for him. I didn't know how much money people would pay for the marijauna, but apparently it was a lot—tens of thousands of dollars. I thought that this was such a blessing for The Family to have enough money to feed The Family better. Money and food were both scarce and greatly needed.

It was getting time to harvest the plants and Sir Knight needed help. Apparently, they had only one day to move fast when the plants were fully-grown. In the meantime, Sir Knight called over to Lanikai to get a few men to help him harvest the plants. They all arrived shortly to help out. Sir Knight trained the brothers on how to harvest the plants—a lot of time and thought went into this project.

The night before harvesting, I made everyone dinner. We all sat outside in our makeshift dining area. I had a bonfire going and the night was warm, with a little breeze. The stars looked so bright at night because there were no lights out. Everyone was so excited for tomorrow's harvest. We all sang around the bonfire and said our blessings for the plants. After dinner and songs, I cleaned up and Sir Knight talked to the brothers to strategize about the next day's activities. By this time, Stardust was fast asleep in the house. We all went to sleep early to get up early.

Sir Knight and the brothers drove to the farm early in the morning before sunrise and were totally shocked to find out— that all the plants were gone! He couldn't believe his eyes. There were hundreds of plants—and now they had all disappeared.

When they returned and told me what happened, I was floored. "How could this have happened?" I thought. Who even knew about the plants, except for Sir Knight and his investor. Unless, perhaps, the investor had put someone up to stealing the crops?

It was so unexpected that the crops would be stolen. I knew that Sir Knight kept everything so confidential even The Family didn't know about the crops. Only a few trusted brothers and the Council Women, who would never jeopardize the income. We never did figure out who stole the crops.

The brothers had only arrived the day before. The farm was in a very remote part of the island. The road was treacherous to drive on. It would have taken an army of trucks to transport so many plants. It was so quiet there that I could hear cars, trucks, or people talking from the house. But on that night, we didn't hear a thing.

This was an awful situation. I had never seen Sir Knight so upset. He had to tell the investor that all his money was lost, and tell The Family that he couldn't generate any money for them. I know that Sir Knight was extremely concerned about telling them. This was horrible and the outcome couldn't be good.

I felt scared after this happened and so did Prism. Once Sir Knight told Makushla and his investor what happened, everything changed. The investor wanted Sir Knight to leave the house and Makushla wanted us all to come back to Lanikai immediately.

I didn't want to leave Sir Knight in such a bad place, but Prism made me go with her. I had become attached to Sir Knight and wanted to stay with him. I reluctantly agreed to go back to Lanikai. Sir Knight drove us to the airport and told me that he would send for me to join him in a week. That it's just temporary. This was good news to me. The next thing I knew, Prism and I were flying back to Oahu to go back home to Lanikai.

I wasn't looking forward to seeing Starman, especially after I snuck out of the house without telling him. I knew he figured out where I was, and with whom, but he never contacted me or Stardust. It was a weird feeling to have no closure with him, and not having communication with his daughter Stardust. That's the way it came down—detachment from me and Stardust. I assumed that maybe he was relieved that we left.

When I got back, Starman wouldn't talk to me. He had another woman and another baby, and gave me the cold shoulder. I went and slept at the Sun Palace with the Council Women. I was confused and in a dilemma if I had done the right thing. But I knew that I didn't have feelings for him anymore. My heart was now with Sir Knight. I knew that Starman loved Stardust but I don't think that he was in love with me any longer. If he was, he would not have let me leave.

The Sun Palace in Lanikai
(me seated at the far right, second row)

Chapter 12

AMONG THE MAYA

Anchor's Yacht

It turned out that Sir Knight had to leave the house and the farm. The investor was so upset that he decided not to fund another project. Sir Knight decided to go back to Los Angeles and work for Anchor (a Family member who was in and out), who was in the pen business. The Family started to disperse and money was getting tight. Going back to Lanikai didn't feel right, to begin with.

Sir Knight sent plane tickets for me and Stardust to fly to Los Angeles. I was so happy he kept his word. It was strange being back at Lanikai and not staying with Starman—we had no closure and it felt so awkward—even though I wanted to keep our relationship as friends, for Stardust's sake. But it seemed like this wasn't going to happen. So I couldn't wait to get to Los Angeles and start a new life.

Sir Knight met me at LAX airport and drove Stardust and me to Marina Del Rey—an upscale harbor where people dock and live on their boats. We were going to live on a yacht owned by Anchor. It was strange to be back in LA after all this time. Now I was eighteen and legal and not worried about the police finding me.

When we arrived at the yacht, I was elated—I loved being out in the ocean and living on a boat seemed exciting. The yacht was a beautiful boat and quite large. Anchor kept it very clean and shiny. There was plenty of room for all of us. On the top level, the captain piloted the boat. On the second level, there were two bedrooms, two bathrooms, a kitchen, and a living room with a big screen television (uncommon at the time), a bar, and a curved couch sitting area.

Most of the time, it was Sir Knight, Stardust and me living there. Anchor lived at his home with his wife and children. Sometimes Anchor would spend the night with us and we would go for long rides out into the ocean. Sometimes we would go to Catalina (an island 26 miles off the LA coast) for days and just chill. It was so much fun. Life on the boat and in LA was nice.

Anchor had a lot of money. He was helping people out in The Family, and was older than everybody else. While many of us were in our teens, he was in his mid-40s. He was super tall—6'5" and seemed to have a heart of gold.

We were free to eat what we wanted (still staying vegetarian) and I could do anything we felt like. This was new to me. I gained almost ten pounds, which was greatly needed after being so emaciated in Hawaii.

At this time, The Source Family started to disperse. Members were not happy with the way the Council Women were handling money and decisions. It was inevitable that The Source Family was coming to an end. Family members would visit us on the boat and tell us stories of The Family not working out. I wasn't surprised.

Afternoons I would walk around the neighborhood with

Stardust. One day I had a grocery bag in one arm, and Stardust in the other, walking down the street close to the Marina. Suddenly I fell and twisted my ankle on a curb. Fortunately Stardust was ok and didn't get hurt, but the groceries fell everywhere. Two policemen in a nearby car saw what happened and came to help me. They drove us all the way to the pier and helped me get to the boat. I appreciated the kindness of strangers.

Every day, I would find something for Stardust and I to do. One afternoon we went to the park down the street from our boat. When Stardust and I returned to the boat, I put her on the ground, as I was trying to get the keys to the yacht out of my pocket. When suddenly, whoops—the keys fell right into the ocean.

In our stretch of the boat slips, we were where all the big yachts were. In this area, not many people actually lived on their boats full-time, and hardly anyone was around the docks in the evening. I waited for what seemed like hours with Stardust for Sir Knight to show up. When he finally did, he had to call divers. And I felt so bad. Two divers eventually came and one went down into the murky water for nearly an hour, as the day grew dark. And at last, they found the keys.

I had a good time living with Sir Knight in the yacht. He was a nice guy and a gentleman. While we were trying to get back into society, there were many transitions and decisions about what to do with my future. One of my decisions—I wanted to go back to school and get a degree. A decision that Sir Knight made was that he wanted to make money growing marijuana. As much as we cared deeply about each other, we clearly had two different directions to go. We were at a pivotal point of deciding what to do—even if we weren't verbally communicating our goals with each other.

Sisters Visit

Two of my sisters (my real sisters) came to visit me in Marina del Rey and took me to dinner at Fisherman's Wharf. They hadn't seen me in years. They wanted to meet Stardust. Then they told me that my mom really wanted to see me and offered me a place to stay, if I needed it.

I hadn't seen my (real) family in about five years. Since I'd run away from home, I had a child, and was 18 now. They had changed so much. I had changed so much. It was strange to see them but comforting at the same time. I was grateful that they wanted to have a relationship with me after what had happened.

When I spoke with them, they wanted to know what had happened with the court case with my mom. When they found out about all the drama, they were completely blown away. They went on to tell me how my mom missed me so much and talked about me all the time. She was devastated when I left. They encouraged me to meet up with my mom.

They said that they thought I looked really good, and they hoped that they could bring my mom and I back together. Interestingly enough, I was welcoming the idea of seeing my mom again. Even though what she did to me was horrible, I was willing to forgive and move on. I thought that this might be the only way that I could have a chance to go to college—was to move back in with my mom. So I decided to explore this possibility.

After seeing my sisters, I started thinking about my future. I was with Sir Knight and living on the boat, but confused about my direction. I was thinking that I would like to go back to school and get a good job, so that I could raise Stardust by myself. It was clear that Starman was not going to be providing for her.

Although I really loved Sir Knight, I didn't get the feeling that we were going to stay together in a long-term relationship. One night, two Family members came to visit us on the yacht—Jupiter and Heaven. When I saw Jupiter again, I had strong feelings for him. He let it be known that he had strong feelings for me as well. He always had a way with words and knew just what to say to me to get me engaged in him.

After this, I could tell that Sir Knight was jealous. I decided to stay behind with Jupiter on the boat, and passed on going to dinner with all of them. That's when Jupiter asked me to come stay with him. For some unknown reason, I decided to take him up on his offer, and go live with him. It was very strange that I would do this, but he had a way with me.

That next day, I packed up all my stuff and Jupiter came and got me. I think I broke Sir Knight's heart. Clearly I was young and stupid. I'm not sure why I left Sir Knight to be with Jupiter. I was in a state of confusion and trying to fit into society again.

Jupiter lived in an apartment off Sunset Boulevard near Laurel Canyon. When Stardust and I lived there, he offered to teach me how to drive and helped me get my driver's license, which I really needed. Up until then, I depended on others to drive me, or I would walk. He let me drive one of his cars. I took the test and passed. Now, for the first time—at the age of 18—I had a driver's license.

The New Norma

I found out from my sisters that my mom now lived in a townhouse in Sherman Oaks. Ironically it was only two blocks away from the Halfway House (at Sepulveda and Magnolia) that I had been sent to a few years earlier.

When we finally met, my mom was, at first, cold and unfriendly. I, in turn, was very distant and unforgiving. She sat in her living room, smoking her cigarette, drinking her glass of wine—barely looking at me or acknowledging Stardust as her grandchild. The first thing she said to me was, "I don't want to be called Grandma." After all, mom had just turned 40. So Stardust would have to call her "Norma."

Stardust was her bubbly friendly self, and was all over my mom. It was very hard for my mom not to accept the cuteness. After she saw me with Stardust, and my interaction with her as a mother, I think that she realized that she needed to forgive and forget. And so did I. My second meeting with her, we talked about me moving back into the house. At this point, I was temporarily living at Jupiter's house.

I decided to move back in with my mom. This seemed to me to be going backwards in life, but instead it was my stepping stone to start my new life. It felt so weird being in her house. She asked me to pay rent and buy my own food. I agreed and didn't want to take advantage of the situation. I was still on welfare and had some money to pay my way. And I knew that I would have to get a job. This was the first time since I ran away from home that I had my own bed (that wasn't on the floor) and my own bathroom. It would take me some time to transition from sleeping on the floor to the bed.

I had a tough time transitioning into this Piscean world. I still was a vegetarian, didn't cut any of my hair, meditated, and thought about Starman a lot. I cried most nights, terrified, wondering if I did the right thing by leaving him. Stardust asked about him often and I would just say that soon she would see him. I didn't know at the time that he and Aura left The Family too and had already moved to Sherman Oaks, close to where my mom lived.

Starman and Aura left The Family shortly after me, and they moved in with Aura's mom back in Los Angeles, in Beverly Glen, up in the hills. Starman found me and we talked and decided to be friends and share parenting responsibilities for Stardust. He never asked me why I left him, but he did ask me if I would ever go back to him. I told Starman that I had moved on and wanted to go back to school and get educated. He seemed to understand and never asked me again.

I was trying to figure things out. How could I make it work with Stardust? I knew that Stardust loved Starman very much. Starman and Stardust looked exactly alike. Meanwhile Starman was married to Aura and they had their daughter Grace.

I was either working or going to take classes at Pierce College—a public community college—in the San Fernando Valley. I had to send Stardust to nursery school full time. She went with Libra, Anastasia's daughter. Several Family members had moved to LA, including Anastasia and Libra—who moved in with her mom. We all became very close. I always needed help picking Stardust up from nursery school. My sisters, Starman, myself—we all took turns picking her up. It was a struggle for a while, but we did make it all work out.

Exploring Love Israel

After The Family dispersed, some people were looking for another commune to join. The Love Israel Family were kind of like our cousins. A lot of my friends had moved to Washington to live with Love Israel. Makushla was one of them—she lived in the house with Love Israel as one of his women. I later found out that Love Israel didn't treat Makushla with the same love and respect as Yahowah did.

After I moved in with my mom, I decided to take a road trip with one of The Source brothers, Hermes, and Stardust. We wanted to check out the Love Israel family—I think we both were searching for a better way of life.

We drove my bright yellow stick-shift Toyota Corolla (I had saved up $2000 from work), taking turns driving up to Washington. After several days of driving, we reached the Love Israel house. We were invited into the main part of the house by Love Israel, and I got a chance to reunite with several Source Family members who had joined them. Everyone in the commune had long hair, and the women wore long dresses. And Love Israel was very religious with the Bible. Not exactly like The Source Family.

We met Love Israel, his two wives, and the rest of the family. We checked it out for the afternoon. We found out that if you joined Love Israel—you couldn't choose who you would be with in a relationship. Love Israel told everyone who to be with. Comparing this to life in The Source Family, this seemed very strict and controlling. After being back in society ("living among the Maya"—as we called the rest of the world outside The Family), I decided I didn't want to be controlled anymore. I liked my freedom to do as I pleased.

We decided to leave and drive back to Los Angeles. But first we went to Tacoma, Washington, where we visited with Paralda and Ocean—who were both in The Source Family. They were living on an orchard farm. We stayed at their house for three nights. Stardust loved being with Paralda and running around the orchard farm picking plums, cherries, and apricots. Since I had to go back to school and finish that semester, Paralda suggested that I leave Stardust there with her.

I don't know what came over me, but I agreed to let Stardust stay there and I agreed that she could stay for two weeks and then Paralda said she would drive home with Stardust to California. That's not exactly what happened—it ended up being over a month until Paralda and Ocean were able to drive Stardust back to California. This was very difficult for me to be away from her. It reminded me of abandonment in my own childhood. This is not the kind of mother that I chose to be, nor did I want to be. However, I was able to get through it and when I reunited with Stardust, I never wanted to be away from her again.

Stardust ended up staying there longer than I expected. She was there for a month and a half. Meanwhile I went back to LA and dove into school. It was the first time for me to be without Stardust. Apparently Stardust was fine and didn't miss me at all. I painfully missed her too much.

Since Stardust was away, I had more freedom to date and work and finish school. I was keeping myself really busy—I was in school full-time (three classes, or fifteen units), and I worked part-time. Now that I was free, I wanted to get back into my passion and love of dance. It was something that made me feel good, and something that I decided to do. Dance class was once a week. I carved out the time for myself.

For five years, when I was in The Source Family, everything that I did was part of the program—and what I was told to do. "Follow the rules." I lost my sense of self in The Source Family. I had to give up any emotions or ego that I might have. That was forbidden. I was not able to think for myself. Everything was decided for me.

I was one of the youngest members in The Source Family (besides the children)—so I fell into the in-between limbo age. Even though some of the Family members were my age—I would assume that they were in the same situation. We never talked to each other about what we were experiencing. It was only later that I found out that they felt the same way.

This dance class was a symbol of my independence. And it also was a return to my roots in dancing. From the age of 8 to 11, I went to Al Gilbert's Theater and Dance Studio, on La Cienega Boulevard in West Hollywood, three or four days a week. I was into tap, jazz, and disco. I was really into it—that was how I was surviving my home family life I lived in at the time. It got me out of the house and out of my head.

Many famous people took lessons at Al Gilbert's Studio, including Michael Jackson and his brothers. I actually danced with Michael Jackson. We were in the same class together. He also went to my middle school (Bancroft Junior High) and sat behind me in math class. My sister dated Jermaine, who was a few years older, and we would go over to their house and hang out. Michael was always really shy. But yes he sure could dance.

During this busy time, I was dating a guy named Michael (not Michael Jackson) who I knew from Fairfax High School. He played bass in a band with my old boyfriend Ronnie in Laurel Canyon. We became very close and had a serious relationship— the first relationship that I had after The Source Family, with someone from outside of The Source Family. While I did not see a future with him, it was a nice relationship.

Around this time, I was at a Source Family get-together in Los Angeles where I saw Pythias. Pythias was the father of my niece, Onka (Amanda) and was my sister's ex-boyfriend in The Family. I thought it might be fun to catch up with him, since we had both been out of The Family for several months, and I was wondering what he was up to.

Pythias asked if he could take me out to dinner. The one evening that I had time was after my once-a-week dance class. Pythias met me after dance class and asked me where I wanted to go eat, and (still being a vegetarian), I suggested that we go to The Aware Inn—which used to be Jim Baker's restaurant and was now owned and operated by his ex-wife Elaine. Pythias agreed.

Déjà Vu

We left my car behind at the dance studio, cruised up La Cienega Boulevard to Sunset Boulevard, and headed to the valet at The

Aware Inn. We walked in through the front door and, to my surprise, the maitre-d' was Bart Baker.

I swear on my life, my body was quivering and my knees gave out on me when I saw him. I was wondering what was going on with me. It felt like a lightning bolt. There was nothing I could have done to stop this overwhelming sensation going through my body.

I hadn't seen Bart for over a year. It was almost a year to the day when Bart was in Hawaii after his Dad passed away. Since that time, we had both been through a lot, on separate paths, and grown up. When Bart saw me, the look on his face was outrageous—pure shock. It was uncontrollable.

Bart sat us at one of the tables downstairs, close to the front entrance of the exclusive gourmet house, so that he could sit down with us, and still pay attention to the clients coming in and out. Bart sat down and joined us for the next two hours. Bart and I were talking non-stop—meanwhile Pythias was sitting there listening to our conversation, not really involved or talking too much. Maybe he had nothing to say. Bart and I were in our own world, reminiscing about the past.

I asked Bart how he was doing, and the first thing Bart told me was that he was engaged to another girl named Wendy. Bart was still 18, and I had just turned 19—I wondered how he could possibly be engaged at that age. But I told him that was exciting and congratulated him. We talked and talked, and never ran out of things to say to each other. Bart took good care of us, and comped us dinner and drinks.

That night we connected so much. Bart asked me, "Can I see you tomorrow for lunch?" Of course I agreed. At the time I was working in Westwood at an organic health food cafe—a little hole in the wall. The next day, Bart drove to Westwood and met me for lunch. On my lunch break, we never actually ate lunch. We just walked and talked and held hands. Obviously there was a connection between us. I used up my whole lunch hour walking and talking to him.

Then after that lunch, Bart called me at my mom's house and asked, "Can we meet again for lunch?" I met him again, and this time it was at The Aware Inn. He offered me a job to work as his assistant part-time. I said yes and started working with him at The Aware Inn upstairs in the office.

Soon after, Stardust returned from Washington and I finally brought her to see Bart. This was really important for me to see how Stardust would respond to him—before I could start a new relationship. As it turned out, Stardust liked him right away. He had just turned 19, but he was so mature for his age. Immediately Stardust embraced Bart with open arms—the loving person that she was, she accepted him right away as my new boyfriend.

As soon as I started dating Bart, Starman became unreliable— not interested and couldn't keep any commitments to Stardust. This was very heartbreaking to Stardust. She would often wait for him for hours on end and he would not show up and not call.

Bart shared many qualities with his dad, Jim. Bart looks like his dad. Same blue eyes. Same face. He was the most amazing gentleman. Kind and gentle to women and people in general. His dad was soft-spoken and had a lot of discipline in his life. They walked alike. They are both hard workers. And they are honest.

It felt like fate being reunited with him. Soon I ended my

relationship with Michael, and Bart ended his relationship with his fiancee. Bart and I started dating again.

When my mom and Bart's mom, Elaine, found out that we were back together, they were shocked. My mom was excited about it. But Bart's mom thought it was a bit weird that I was back again, now with a child from a former Family member, from her ex-husband's commune. But we were obviously in love and undeterred.

Raising Stardust

After The Source Family commune, I met Bart again and he and I dated for the next two years, very happy although with very little money, but very much in love. This was the first time in my life that I felt love, like I have never felt before.

At this time in my life I was very insecure and unsure of myself. I wasn't sure I was capable of loving another person or capable of accepting love from another person. Throughout my relationship with Bart for the next two years, I learned that I can love and I can be loved. I had no idea what it was like to commit fully to another person until I met Bart.

Bart proposed to me on Christmas Eve in 1977. We were at home with Stardust at the time, opening presents. And I of course said *yes*. Later, when I told Starman that Bart and I were getting married, he wasn't happy about this. Once Starman knew this was the real thing, he started showing absolutely no interest in his daughter Stardust. He became very irresponsible towards her. Bart ended up picking up the father role and we both decided that after we were married and settled down that we would start the adoption process. We didn't want Starman to be able to take Stardust away from me.

It took a while to convince Starman this was the right thing to do—and it wasn't easy. But eventually he agreed and signed the adoption papers. And she never saw him again until she was 21 years old. I'm sure Stardust was hurt that he didn't fight for her. I know this causes emotional stress. I also think that Starman didn't really think this through and possibly regretted doing so.

In hindsight, it was the right thing for him to do. Bart was a great dad to Stardust and was there for her emotionally, mentally, and physically all the time. She was his daughter and he treated her like she was his own.

Stardust became an incredible person—she was a great student, accomplished athlete, amazing dancer, very popular, kind, great big sister, very-community oriented, a champion swimmer, and she became a lifeguard and a cheerleader. Stardust would wake up early in the morning at 4:30 a.m. and start working out to a Jazzercise video on TV. The whole house would be rocking on the second floor and we always knew it was Stardust dancing and exercising to the music. She played the violin and the viola. She was in Chair #2 on viola for the Malibu Middle School orchestra and performed in a competition at Disneyland. She also played in *Stairway to the Stars* during high school.

Stardust was dedicated to her swimming—she was a champion swimmer at Malibu Middle School and broke many records. She also became a champion swimmer at Santa Monica High School. In order to get into the pool by 6 a.m., she would wake up at 4:30 a.m., get dressed on her own, make her own lunches, walk in the dark about 10 blocks to the bus (she knew the bus driver by name) and she would catch the bus to get to Santa Monica High School by 6 a.m. to jump in the pool and do the workout.

Whatever she did, Stardust was dedicated and did it to the fullest, always with a smile. She was the happiest, most positive child I have ever known. When Stardust decided to go to college, she chose to go to Chico State University. However Chico State University did not have a football team and this did not sit well with Stardust. So she decided to go to Butte Junior College in Chico, CA where they had a football team, basketball team, and a baseball team—and try out for the cheerleading squad. Not surprisingly, she got accepted to be on the cheerleading team. Once again Stardust was doing what she loved—dancing and cheering for the football and baseball teams.

Stardust went to college to become a teacher, which was her goal. She transferred to Northridge State University halfway through Butte and joined the Valley Masters Swim Club at Northridge. This is where she met her future husband Jason who was also in the Masters Swim program.

When Stardust was interning to be a teacher in the inner city of Los Angeles, she taught a class and she became so emotionally involved in the abuse that these children had, that she wanted to bring every child home to me and have them come live with us and for me to take care of them. This didn't work out very well, and she decided she could not be a teacher.

Today Stardust is married to her college sweetheart Jason. They have been married for over 20 years and they have two twin ten-year-old boys, Jonah and Jake. Stardust became a spe-cial-needs assistant teacher. This is what she loves and this is what her calling is and how she gives back to her community.

The Greatest Love

My relationship with Bart was rekindled at the age of 19—we got married at the age of 21. We had two more children after Stardust—Amber and Brian. We have been married for 44 years. Every day I am with Bart, I am so happy and in total bliss. Together we have raised three beautiful children and we now have four grandsons. It seems to me that we were meant to be from day one.

I never did finish college and get that education that I so wish I had. But I did get an incredible education in a spiritual sense from Father and The Source Family commune. This education taught me how to get through life's hardships and how to use my skills to overcome anything.

My time in The Source Family was so invaluable to me. To this day, I continue to use the nutritional tools that were taught to me, as well as the breathing techniques with meditation. Because Bart understood what I went through in The Source Family, he was able to help me get through a lot of my emotional stress. My marriage to Bart is the best decision I've ever made in my life. My children are the most beautiful reflection of our love for them.

I know I didn't have a conventional life as a youth, but I am truly blessed to have experienced what I did in The Source Family. I love my brothers and my sisters to this very day. They all mean so much to me and we've all been through so much together. I guess you can say I came full circle. It all started when I met Bart at 12 years old and then came back to him at 19. Whatever our past lives experienced, we have the greatest love story of all.

Wendy (me), Bart, and Stardust

EPILOGUE

Reflections

Today as I'm writing this book about my journey as a youth, I've learned more about myself than I thought possible. I was transformed by my time in The Source Family (for the most part) from the age of 14-19 years old. I am convinced, more than ever now, that I needed to leave my Earth family. I was so depressed growing up and I wasn't sure why. I had no one to talk to, to express my inner feelings. I just knew that if I stayed in this situation, I would end up with deep emotional problems.

When I met Jim Baker and he was so magnetic and full of love—I was immediately attracted to him. I had never felt this way before. My body and soul gravitated towards Jim Baker without me really knowing it. It was like I was being guided by my guardian angels to leave my home and go on a different path. It was so strong that I was blindsided by the consequences.

What I learned from Jim Baker, Father, Yahowah, was how to live and how to love. He taught me the power of meditation and discipline. I did the Mystic Road twice. It helped to develop in me a strong inner peace. I learned how to eat organic healthy vegetarian foods. I learned that there is power in nutritional foods.

Hatha yoga was a big part of The Source teachings. I learned that there is power in the breath. The first time I did the Star Exercise I passed out. Today I use this powerful exercise to refresh my soul.

I knew I needed to purify my body and Yahowah taught us how to fast and eliminate the poisons in our bodies, which I still do to this day. Yahowah's philosophy of eating, exercise, discipline, relationships, and the power of positive thinking will be forever ingrained in my soul. Even though he went off on some other path, the foundation taught to me in the beginning stuck with me. Yahowah believed that we could live in perfect harmony together as a spiritual family and survive all the negativity in the world. It almost worked. It did work until he died and that perfect harmony died with him.

I did question Yahowah a lot in my mind. I always gave Yahowah my one hundred percent faith in him. I was young and constantly learning from Yahowah's teachings. I gave myself completely to Yahowah. I loved him like a father. When I was with Yahowah I always felt like I was the only one there. In my story you can read that I trusted Yahowah with my life. Looking back I am amazed at the faith I had at such a young age. I realize that I became a stronger person than I was before The Family.

I realized that I had to stay in The Family due to my legal status. After what Yahowah jeopardized his life for—saving my life in the court legal system—I was eternally grateful that he rescued me. His plan was genius and worked. No one ever before had risked their life to help me with anything. I realized later that if Yahowah hadn't rescued me from the legal system, I would have ended up in foster care. This would have taken me to a completely different path. One that I didn't want to go to.

The whole time I was in The Source Family it felt like spiritual bootcamp. Things were constantly changing and I needed to go with the flow. Because if I didn't, I would not survive. Life was strict and monitored often—by either Yahowah, the Family elders, or any of the Family members. They didn't hesitate to call you out when you were not following the rules.

I'm still not sure today if I was happy there. I may have been so busy trying to keep up with everything that I didn't have time to be happy. I have always tried to be perfect in whatever I needed to do. So when it came time for me, there wasn't any time. I never wanted to get into trouble and noticed. I was busy trying to survive. In The Family it was better to blend in than to stand out and be a firecracker. I was a "blender." I was quiet and mostly observed.

I wanted to learn as much as possible so I could be an excellent follower. It was like when I was a student in school. I strived to be the best and learn as much as I could.

What lessons I didn't take with me are: Now, I cut my hair and dye it. I am no longer a vegetarian, but I don't eat meat—only poultry and fish. I wake up at 6:30 a.m. instead of 4:30 a.m. and I wear many different styles of clothing. I am in a long term monogamous relationship of 44 years, married to Jim Baker's son Bart. I have three beautiful children—Jaime aka Stardust, Amber and Brian. I also have four grandsons, Julian, Luca, Jonah and Jacob. I live in a Piscean world and I'm probably on an ego trip, whatever that really means.

I've been married to the most amazing man, Bart, who

inherited his parents' best qualities and is my hero. Bart understands me to the fullest and accepts me for who I am. He knows everything I've been through and still loves me, for better or for worse. I am the luckiest woman alive. I am grateful to Jim and Elaine for raising such a beautiful person. Yahowah prepared me for this incredible relationship.

The Best Idea

Running away from home and joining a commune—maybe was not the best idea? But being in juvenile hall made me want to be in The Source Family even more. People were there in The Family for different reasons—from my perspective. Spiritual seeking. Friendships. Lonely. The girls and the sex. And some were hiding from getting drafted to fight in Vietnam. Some for the food. Some for communal living. Some people didn't have their financial trip together—so they could live there and have things taken care of. I was there because of my love for Father and I was also looking for a loving family life.

When The Family split up—whatever people were doing before—it seemed they went back to it. Like me, I decided to go back to school and finish my degree. There are people who are still living by Yahowah's teachings. They have a pyramid mirror in their house, they meditate while chanting his name, and still believe the way we did back then.

We were the hippie side of the sex, drugs, and rock n' roll. Our version of "Sex, Drugs, Rock 'n' Roll" was "Dhyanism, Sacred Herb, and Ya Ho Wah 13 band." In some ways, we epitomized communal living in the 1970s. We followed the Essene Gospel teachings, as well as teachings from many different places—whatever sounded good to Yahowah—for the "movie" that day. It was constantly changing.

Being in The Source Family saved my life—it made me a better person. I take nothing for granted. I am not attached to material things. I am grateful for what I have. My heart is with anyone who was in The Source Family. We all went through so much together, and could never forget. It was my fraternity and sorority. It was far out and way out. It gave me an adventure to talk about and to remember.

I did miss graduating high school, like most people my age. I never went to the prom. I had a child and I couldn't experience partying. Did I miss out? Or did I escape this nonsense? I'll never know because I didn't have that. However I did watch my children have all the experiences of normal youths. I found it fascinating and today I'm okay without having this in my life. It took a while to be okay with missing out.

At first I was saddened, and regretted it. Today I realize that I was destined to go the path of spiritual being. I have used my skills while raising my children. I taught them many techniques, like how to breathe when stressed or in pain. I also instilled healthy eating habits as children. They ate only organic foods and stayed away from sugar. Today they make their own choices. At first I raised Stardust vegetarian, but later on she chose to eat meat. And that's okay. I also taught them the power in thinking positive thoughts and thinking independently.

My children are Jim Baker's grandchildren. They have his genes and are already on a spiritual path. My daughter Amber inherited Yahowah's gift of channeling. She can connect with the

Akashic Records and the Council of Twelve. Amber has thousands of followers and is teaching her clients how to channel the Akashic Records. My son Brian has the strong Baker quality of confidence and nutritional habits. He also has a love of music. Stardust has the power of positive thinking. She's always happy no matter what's going on. Stardust really is a Saint.

I have never told my children what happened to me in The Source Family. They are also learning about my experiences for the first time as they read this book. They have given me their blessings to write this book and tell my story to the world. The only person I told all my stories to is Bart Baker, my husband of 44 years. I am so appreciative to him for not judging me and always supporting me. He is my biggest support in writing this true story. He has the best qualities of Jim Baker. He inherited the good genes and received the best of Jim Baker's teachings as a young child. So you put these two parents together and you get three amazing children of incredible qualities.

Think For Yourself

The downfall of The Source philosophy was that people couldn't think for themselves. And Yahowah paid for it with his life. This thought process always used the expression: "If it's meant to be, so be it." Which to me seemed to take away my responsibility for the outcome. Instead of the choices that I make, I own them, and I'm responsible for the outcomes.

Some people in The Family did think for themselves. Early on at The Mother House, Magus's baby had a high fever and we couldn't get it down. So Magus left The Family and got his baby medical attention. Like Anastacia, choosing to take her baby Libra to the hospital and get medical attention. Also Sunflower for making the decision to take Aura to the hospital after she gave birth to Grace. This may have saved both Aura and baby Grace's lives. This was a big lesson for me to learn. With those actions, who knows—maybe Jim wanted us to ultimately pass that test.

Thinking for yourself was considered an "ego trip"—anything that wasn't perfect within the margins of selfless acts. The few members in The Family that did think for themselves either left The Family early or made their own decisions after Yahowah passed away. Not everyone followed Yahowah's philosophy of only seeking Western medical attention if you broke a bone. This is not my philosophy today. Today I believe in getting both modern medical attention and Eastern.

I loved my brothers and sisters in The Source Family. We all had been through a lot together. For whatever reason, they joined The Family. We all experienced a path of spirituality, friendship, Love and the art of communal living. Those of us who stuck it out to the end became the strength.

Forgiveness

One of the most important lessons was that I learned to forgive. When The Source dispersed and all my brothers and sisters had to fit into Society again, I needed to make amends with my Earth Mother, Norma. This was the hardest thing so far. But it was so necessary in order for me to move on.

When I first saw my mother, I was so angry and had no way of forgiving her. After time went on, I realized that she did the best she could. She had given birth to four girls from a man who wasn't supportive and was drunk all the time. Her parents disowned her and she was on her own, a single parent. I'm sure that we four girls reminded her of her abusive drunk husband daily. I also know that her parents never let her forget her mistake.

My mother and I learned to forgive each other as I slowly earned her trust again. It became my mission to show her that I loved her. In return, she eventually forgave me for running away. It wasn't easy for her, but we ended up becoming so close. She was my biggest supporter in everything I did. Always cheering me on with all of my responsibilities and goals in life.

It took her a long time to say she loved me. In fact she even eventually started hugging me. At first I withdrew from her hugs. Then I got used to it and we always hugged goodbye. This was big for her. She loved her grandchildren more than her own. I was okay with this because I knew it gave her a second chance.

My mom and I had an understanding to not talk about the past and what we did to hurt each other. I also did not ever talk about my life in The Source Family. She never asked me about my experience in the Halfway House or how I escaped. This was unspoken.

In the end I took care of my mom. All of her needs were met. My sister Marci, aka Blessing, became her caregiver for two years of devotion. She needed love and care and for me to take over her responsibilities of everyday life. She put her trust in me and wanted me to make all of her medical and financial decisions. I took this very seriously. I don't think all of my sisters were okay with this. But this is what she wanted from me.

She put her complete trust in me. For this I am thankful

that I was able to show her my love. It became so healing for both of us. Now I know that we forgive each other and show the ultimate love and trust. I am a better person today for having this experience. Her last words to me were, "Wendy I love you." In her strong voice. Forgiveness.

"GO": Me and Starman pictured at the far right,
first row (standing)

"So mote it be."—*Father Yahowah*

At The Father House: Father Yod,
Starman (holding baby Onka), Pythias, and Rain

"Showing the Way" ~ Me on the far right
(credit: Isis Aquarian)

Jim Baker and Yogi Bhajan
During our Sikh religion times

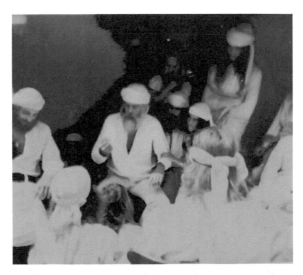

Father speaking at The Source Restaurant

Me holding a baby at The Source Restaurant
(credit for both photos: Zain Korngute)

*Meditation in The Source Restaurant parking lot
on Sunset Boulevard
(credit: Zain Korngute)*

*Gathering at The Source Restaurant
(credit: Zain Korngute)*

Father and his followers
(credit: Zain Korngute)

Waterfall, Pythias, (unknown), and Serenity
(credit: Zain Korngute)

*Me and Aqauriana—group massages
at The Source Restaurant
(credit: Zain Korngute)*

*Starman, Sancia (holding baby Gallahad), Waterfall
(credit: Zain Korngute)*

The Family at The Mother House

Father—early stages of The Family
(credit: Zain Korngute)

Painting of the Star Exercise

Wedding Day—July 2, 1978
Me, Bart, and Stardust

Me and Bart—2022

Bart and Me—2022

Me and my daughter Amber Baker—2022

*Amanda (Onka), Celeste (Tau—Jim Baker's daughter),
and Jaime (Stardust)—all born in The Source Family*

Bart Baker and Celeste Baker—2022

*Sarah and Brian Baker's
wedding day—2022*

Family vacation—Turtle Island, Fiji

Patti Palafox and Amber Baker—married

Jaime (Stardust) and husband Jason

Brian Baker, Amber Baker,
Jaime Baker with Elaine Baker—2017

Ben Baker and Bart Baker—2022

Me and my mom Norma Gossard—2017

Marci (Blessing), Elizabeth (Paralda), and me

Marci (Blessing)   *Me and Nancy (Heaven)—2022*

Nirvana (me) and Mate (my sister)
Morning meditation at The Source

my name was mushroom

My Life as a Teenage Runaway
in The Source Family Commune

wendy baker & brian solon

Wendy Baker
(credit: Jack Guy)

ABOUT THE AUTHOR

Wendy Baker is an author and entrepreneur. With her husband, Bart Baker, she runs an insurance agency. In her spare time, she volunteers at the Lighthouse Women's and Children's Shelter in Oxnard, California. She's passionate about helping teenage mothers succeed in life. Wendy lives in Malibu, California, with her husband and enjoys spending time with their three grown children and four grandchildren.

Made in United States
Troutdale, OR
11/15/2023